Getting To Know...

Nature's Children

SEALS

Merebeth Switzer

SCHOLASTIC INC.

New York Toronto London Auckland Sydney
Mexico City New Delhi Hong Kong Buenos Aires

Facts in Brief

Classification of North American earless seals

Class: *Mammalia* (mammals)

Order: *Carnivora* (meat-eaters)

Family: *Phocidae* (seal family)

Genus and species: 13 genera and 18 species around the world; most common in North America: Harbor Seal, Harp Seal, Ringed Seal, Bearded Seal, Gray Seal, Hooded Seal, Northern Elephant Seal

World Distribution. Seals are found throughout the Polar regions, and as far south as California and New York in North America, Wales in Europe, and Japan in Asia.

Habitat. Usually live where ocean water meets land or solid ice; may move into fresh water; some migrate in search of food.

Distinctive Physical Characteristics. Has no external ears, simply openings on side of head; rear flippers cannot be turned forward; coarse stiff coat with no underfur.

Diet. Mainly fish but also various other sea animals.

Published by Scholastic Inc.
90 Old Sherman Turnpike, Danbury, Connecticut 06816.

SCHOLASTIC and associated logos are trademarks of Scholastic Inc.

ISBN 0-7172-6696-6   Printed in the U.S.A.

Edited by: Elizabeth Grace Zuraw   *Photo Editor:* Nancy Norton
Photo Rights: Ivy Images   *Cover Design:* Niemand Design

Have you ever wondered . . .

What barks like a dog, has whiskers like a cat, and swims like a fish? If you guessed a seal, congratulations! Seals have an unusual combination of features that equip them for life on land as well as in the water. They're one of the few animals that are at home in both worlds.

When people think about seals, they often picture performing seals. But most of the animals that perform in zoos and marine parks are not seals, they're Sea Lions.

The seal, nonetheless, is a superb swimmer, and it can put on a flashy show of its own. It can perform a combination of spins, twirls, and somersaults, then disappear below the water's surface in an amazing speed dive.

On land, seals are not as graceful as they are in the water. But they seem to enjoy sunbathing and "talking" to friends, much as human vacationers do at a beach.

A Harbor Seal rests on a sandy shore. Harbor Seals stay close to home, seldom venturing more than 10 miles from where they were born.

Inquisitive Pups

The sleek, smooth body of a pudgy young seal skims through the water of a harbor. Suddenly the baby seal, called a *pup,* stops and pops its head up to check its surroundings. Its large brown eyes focus on a sailboat quietly gliding by. Overcome by curiosity, the pup watches while bobbing closer to the strange object. Then all at once, a huge flapping sail unfurls on the boat. The pup dives fast—and deep—into the water. Even though the young adventurer is curious, it'll leave *this* giant sea monster alone!

A young seal's playful curiosity disappears as it grows up and becomes more cautious about the world around it. Such watchfulness is important. In order to survive, the pup must learn to be wary of its surroundings.

Gray Seal pups are white at birth. As adults, Gray Seals vary in color from pale gray to nearly black. Females often are lighter than the males.

Fin-footed Families

There are many different kinds of seals. They all belong to a group of animals called *pinnipeds,* which means "fin-footed." You have only to look at these animals' large, flipper-like feet to know why scientists have given them this name. And flippers are very useful to a seal. When a creature spends as much time in the water as pinnipeds do, flippers are much more practical than ordinary feet.

Eared seal

The pinniped group is made up of three families—walruses, eared seals (which include Sea Lions and fur seals), and earless seals, often called true seals. The earless seal family is the biggest and most widespread of the three pinniped families. There are 18 kinds of earless seals and about half of them are found in North America.

Earless seal

A fur seal belongs to the eared seal family. In this photo, the small earflaps are clearly visible on either side of the seal's head.

Seal or Sea Lion?

It's not surprising that people sometimes get seals and Sea Lions confused. But if you look closely, you'll notice some differences.

First look at the ears. Sea Lions have ears that are easy to see. They belong to the group of seals called eared seals. Although true seals have ears, too, their ears are only tiny openings on the sides of their heads. They don't have earflaps as Sea Lions do.

Both seals and Sea Lions are beautifully streamlined for life in the water, but their hind flippers are quite different. As a result, the two animals swim and move on land in different ways. Sea Lions can walk and even run on land because they can stand on their hind flippers. In the water they paddle with their large front flippers and steer with their back flippers. Seals use their hind flippers as a huge fin to do most of the swimming work.

On land, a seal's hind flippers are of little use. Instead of walking, a seal wiggles along like an overgrown caterpillar.

Opposite page: It's hard to find the tiny ear openings on an earless, or true, seal.

Seal front flipper

Sea Lion front flipper

Creature of Two Worlds

The seal is a creature of two worlds—water and land. In water, it moves with grace and ease. And unlike most aquatic animals, it can move from salt water to fresh water if the need arises.

At the same time, the seal is a *mammal,* and one feature of a mammal is that it has lungs and it needs to breathe air. That need takes the seal ashore, where it also goes to rest and to *mate,* or produce young.

From the Arctic *ice floes*—large floating pieces of flat ice—to the rocky shores of Newfoundland and the sandy beaches of California, the seal lives in areas where water meets land and solid ice.

Opposite page:
A baby Harp Seal is quite at home in its frozen world of ice and snow.

In North America, seals can be found as far south as New York on the Atlantic Coast, and all the way down to California and Mexico on the Pacific Coast.

13

Watery Wonder

A seal is wonderfully suited to its watery existence. Its sleek, torpedo-shaped body glides easily through the water and helps make the animal an excellent swimmer.

Seals are remarkable in their ability to remain underwater for long periods of time— 20 minutes or more. How do they manage?

Before a seal dives, it breathes out all the air in its lungs. That makes diving easier and safer because the intense pressure found in deep water doesn't affect a seal if it has no air in its lungs. But the seal's heart and brain, like yours, need *oxygen*—the part of the air that is used by the body. Like you, the seal can get oxygen only from air. Unlike you, however, all the oxygen the seal needs underwater is contained in its blood. Until the seal comes to the surface again to breathe, most of the oxygen in the seal's blood goes to its most important body organs—the heart and brain.

Seals are world-class swimmers.

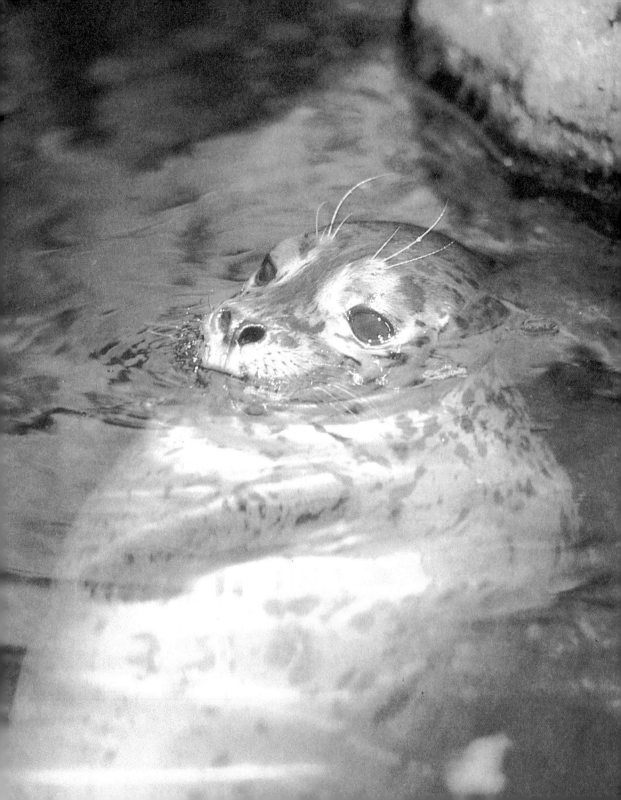

Diving Champs

Scuba divers must really envy seals. Without special equipment, human divers can go to a depth of only 150 feet (45 meters). Diving any deeper is dangerous. But many seals can dive twice as deep as a human. And some of these diving champs, such as the Elephant Seal, can reach depths of about 1,000 feet (300 meters)!

Your heart beats about 72 times a minute. A seal's heart normally beats much faster, about 150 times per minute. But when the seal dives, its heart rate drops to 60 beats per minute. On very deep or long dives, its heartbeat may drop as low as 10 to 20 beats a minute. By having its heart pump blood much more slowly, the seal can make the supply of oxygen in its blood last longer.

When it comes up for air, a seal breathes through its nostrils. But when the seal dives, the nostrils close.

Big, Beautiful Brown Eyes

A seal's large brown eyes have special features to help the animal see underwater. Because it can be very dark deep down in the ocean, the *pupils,* or inner circles, of a seal's eyes open extra wide to let in more light. Out of the water in bright sunlight, the pupils shrink to a tiny slit.

If you've ever kept your eyes open while swimming in the ocean, then you know that salt water soon makes your eyes sting. Seals don't have this problem. They have an extra, transparent eyelid that they can pull over their eyes to protect them when underwater.

Finally, seals do a lot of crying—but not because they're sad! Seals can't control the tears that flow from their eyes. Just as your eyes water in order to wash away specks of dust, seals' tears flow freely to wash away anything that might irritate their eyes.

A baby Harp Seal is called a whitecoat. *But when it grows up, it'll have a gray coat and a dark pattern on its back shaped like a harp, a curved musical instrument. Can you guess how Harp Seals got their name?*

Sizing Up Seals

Most types of seals range from 3 to 6 feet (1 to 2 meters) in length, and weigh from 200 to 500 pounds (90 to 225 kilograms). But male Northern Elephant Seals can grow to more than 20 feet (6 meters) in length, and weigh as much as 8,000 pounds (3,600 kilograms). That's longer than most people's living rooms and heavier than two cars! In fact, the Elephant Seal is one of the largest creatures on Earth.

As is the case with many animals, the males, or *bulls,* are often much bigger than the females, or *cows.*

Take a look at the huge nose and massive size of this animal. It's not hard to see how the Elephant Seal got its name!

A Blanket of Blubber

Imagine hopping into a bathtub full of freezing water and blocks of ice. Brrr! You'd feel like a human icicle just seconds after you plunged in! Not so with seals. They can spend long periods of time swimming in water that's often part ice. How do seals manage this chilly feat? They're protected by *blubber,* a thick layer of body fat under their skin. A seal's blubber can be up to 6 inches (15 centimeters) thick. This bountiful blanket of blubber acts as insulation, keeping a seal's body heat in and the cold out.

Blubber also helps to smooth out the seal's body shape, making it even more streamlined for swimming. And because blubber is light, it helps keep the seal afloat. The seal doesn't need to work so hard when swimming.

A seal finds its blubber very useful in another way, too. When necessary, the seal can go for weeks without eating, drawing the energy it needs from the blubber stored on its body.

From one-third to nearly one-half of an
adult seal's weight consists of blubber.

Air-conditioning Flippers

Believe it or not, a seal is kept so warm by its layer of blubber that it sometimes gets overheated! Since the seal can't take off its blubber blanket when it gets hot, the animal has come up with another way to cool off. It gets rid of extra heat through its flippers.

The seal's flippers aren't covered with blubber. Instead, they're crisscrossed with blood vessels, When a seal gets too warm, it can pump large amounts of blood through its flippers. There the blood is cooled by the surrounding air or water. The cooled blood then returns to the rest of the body and soon the seal's temperature goes back to normal.

Telltale Teeth

The teeth and claws of seals are made up of layers, like tree rings. A new layer is added every year. By counting the layers, scientists can tell a seal's age. Some seals live 25 years or more in the wild.

The seal's natural enemies include Polar Bears, Killer Whales, sharks, and occasionally, wolves. Young seals are particularly vulnerable, especially during their first weeks of life. A Golden Eagle, walrus, or other large predator considers a baby seal an easy meal. A *predator* is an animal that hunts other animals for food.

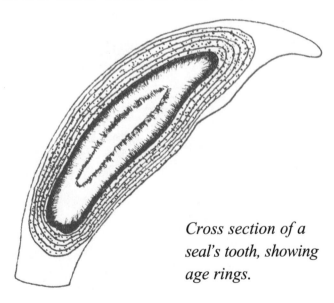

Cross section of a seal's tooth, showing age rings.

Who Are You?

To us, most seals look a lot alike. It's difficult to tell one from another. Seals seem to have the same problem we do. On a crowded beach they don't seem to be able—just by looking— to tell their own babies from other babies, or friends from strangers.

Instead, seals use smell and sound to help them identify one another. Most seals have a keen sense of smell. A mother seal uses it to recognize her own baby. This is very important if she's in a large group with other seals and their young.

Seals also use a wide range of calls to find a friend in a crowd. These "Who are you?" calls vary with the type of seal. Some seals make grunting and squeaking sounds, while others make dog-like barks.

Hooded Seals, found in the North Atlantic, are pale gray with black blotches and spots.

Seals—Together and Alone

When you think of seals, you may think of large groups of them clustered together on a beach. Or you may think of just a few seals playing together.

Many seals do live in groups. Some of them gather when they're ashore, but go their separate ways when they return to the water to feed. Others, such as the Harp Seal, spend all of their time in groups. During *mating season*—the time of year during which the seals come together to produce young—and while moving from one place to another, a group of Harp Seals may number in the thousands.

But there are other kinds of seals that prefer to live alone. The Ringed Seal, in particular, spends nearly all of its time on its own. The mother gives birth to one baby in a secluded *den,* or animal home, which she digs under snow or in a natural hollow in the ice. Mother and baby stay together for about two months. Except for this family-raising time, however, and a brief time spent with a partner during mating season, the Ringed Seal remains alone.

A herd of Harp Seals shares an icy realm. Social creatures, these seals prefer to live in groups rather than alone.

Seal-time Meal-time

Since seals search for food in the water, you can probably guess what one of their favorite foods is. That's right—fish.

But seals eat other foods as well. Harbor Seals search for small sea creatures in *tide pools,* patches of water left behind by the outgoing tide. The ocean-roaming Harp Seal eats small fish such as herring and capelin and masses of tiny, shrimp-like shellfish called *krill.*

Many seals prefer to eat bottom-living sea animals such as crabs, clams, whelks, shrimp, snails, and octopuses. In fact, a Bearded Seal has special whiskers like a walrus to help it search for tasty treats on the dark ocean bottom. Scientists think that the seal rakes up the bottom with its front claws and then uses its whiskers to sift through the debris. When the Bearded Seal finds a yummy whelk or succulent clam, it uses its strong jaws and teeth to crush the shell to get at the food. Since it doesn't need the shell in its diet, the seal spits out the broken pieces.

Opposite page: *A seal's whiskers are sensitive feelers that help the animal find food in the murky ocean depths.*

Long Journeys

Opposite page:
*A baby Harp Seal
grows fast. By
two weeks, it is
swimming and
eating fish.*

You probably know that many birds *migrate*—
they travel south every fall, then north again in
the spring. But did you know that some seals
do the same thing? When winter comes, seals
that live in large groups in Arctic waters must
migrate south to find food.

Harp Seals probably are the best known
migrators. In summer, when northern waters
teem with small fish and tiny sea animals,
Harp Seals live and feed in the cold water at
the edge of the Arctic's *pack ice*—the ice formed
by the crashing together of chunks of ice. In the
fall as the temperature goes down, the ice begins
to spread southward over the seals' feeding
grounds. The seals then have to move further
south to stay ahead of the ice. Harp Seals migrate
as much as 2,000 miles (3,200 kilometers) to
their southern feeding grounds. When spring
returns and the sun warms the air, the seals head
north again, following the ice's melting edge.

Not all kinds of seals migrate. Those that
live alone or in small groups don't make such
long journeys.

Birth Time

Baby seals may be born at different times of the year, depending on which type of seal they are and where their home is. Most seal mothers, however, give birth in late winter. They haul themselves out onto the ice or onto land to have their babies.

Some cows gather in large groups to have their babies; others give birth alone. In either case, the bulls usually stay away from the females at this time. They may form bachelor groups or go off by themselves. They don't help care for the babies after they're born.

Where there's a seal pup this young, the mother probably isn't far away.

Meet the Baby

Seal babies are quite small compared to their mothers. Ringed Seal babies may weigh as little as 10 pounds (4.5 kilograms), while Bearded Seal pups may weigh as much as 80 pounds (36 kilograms.)

Most seals that are born on ice or snow have a soft, woolly white coat. A baby's coat is very important because it will keep the newcomer warm until its body has a chance to build up a layer of blubber. A white coat also helps the pup blend into its snowy home so that it's not easily spotted by predators.

Seals that are born on cliffs or sandy beaches are usually a dark brown or mottled color that matches their surroundings. Such a matching of colors, called *camouflage,* helps to hide and protect the young seals on the rocky or sandy beaches where they spend the first weeks of their life.

A Harbor Seal pup is usually born with a spotted coat very much like its mother's, except a little lighter in color.

A Caring Mother

A baby seal begins to *nurse,* or drink milk from its mother's body, minutes after it is born. Some babies nurse in the water; others do so on land or on ice floes. A mother seal's milk is so thick and rich that it looks like soft creamy butter.

A baby seal doesn't spend a long time with its mother, but while it is with her, it's well cared for. A mother seal stays near her baby, ready for its almost constant demands to nurse. If she does leave for any reason, she's seldom gone long.

Female Harbor Seals are ready to start a family when they're four years old. Males mature at five years of age.

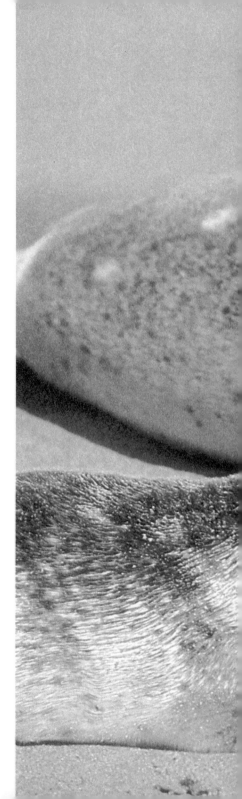

Swimming Lessons

Seals are natural swimmers, but this doesn't mean that a baby seal jumps right into the water. This strange new wetness requires a close checking out before the first plunge is taken. The curious pup creeps up to the water's edge, and after a sniff and a sidelong glance, it plops itself into the water. There the flustered baby bobs about, unsure of its new surroundings. Soon, though, it'll be swimming with the same ease and grace as its mother. When it needs a rest, a tired pup may hitch a ride on its mother's shoulders.

Hooded Seal pups are called bluebacks *because of their blue-tinged fur.*

A Hasty Departure

Some pups have two months or more of their mother's care, but many are left to fend for themselves when they're only about two weeks old. Still, these pups are well prepared for life on their own. They're already at home in the water, and most have grown-up teeth for feeding. In other words, they have all the tools they need to survive. They simply need to learn how to use them. And until they do learn to catch their own food, they can live off the blubber on their bodies.

There are reasons for the mother seal's rather hasty departure. If she is to have another baby the next year, she needs to seek out a male partner with whom she can mate. Also, the seal cow hasn't eaten since giving birth. In supplying milk for her baby, she has used up a great deal of her body fat. If she's to survive, mate, and have another baby, she must soon stop nursing her youngster.

Mating Time

Mating usually takes place a few weeks after the cows have left their pups. At this time the cows and bulls actively seek out each other. Some bulls put on spectacular swimming displays to impress a female, and often two bulls will fight each other to determine who will father the young.

Among some types of seals, a powerful bull may gather a *harem,* or group of several cows. He'll mate with the cows in his harem and protect them from the advances of other males. At first he'll probably just try to discourage an intruding male by lowering his head and hissing. If that doesn't work, he'll fight. Usually the intruder gives up and leaves before anyone is seriously hurt.

During mating season, some male seals give off a powerful musky odor. As unappealing as this smell may be to a human nose, it works just fine to attract female seals.

Opposite page: Within two to three weeks of birth, a Gray Seal pup sheds its coat of creamy-white fur. The coat is replaced by a much darker one, similar to that of its parents.

New Coats for Old

After adult seals mate, they *molt,* or shed their coats. By this time their old coats are ragged and shaggy. They've been worn away in many spots over the last year. In some cases, the coats shed in large pieces, sometimes taking old, dead outer skin with them.

While they're molting, seals rest and remain on land. They don't eat. Instead, they live off their stores of blubber. But within a few weeks, the bulls and cows have grown new coats of coarse fur.

It's now time to return to the ocean for their first meal in a long time. The seals eagerly head out in search of food. Most of the seals will live out in the ocean until the next spring when they'll again haul themselves out onto the land or ice where the next generation of pups will be born.

Seals have a fairly long life span—if they can overcome the risks they face both in the water and on land. Eared seals live to about 18 years of age. Earless seals live about 25 years.

Words To Know

Blubber Layer of fat on an animal's body that keeps body heat in.

Bull A male seal.

Camouflage Animal features that blend in with its surroundings.

Cow A female seal.

Den An animal home.

Harem A group of females that a bull mates with and protects.

Ice floes Large floating pieces of flat ice.

Krill Tiny, shrimp-like shellfish.

Lungs The organ of the body that takes oxygen from the air and makes it available to the rest of the body.

Mammal An animal that breathes air, is warm-blooded, is born live, drinks its mother's milk, and has some kind of hair during some stage of its life.

Mate To come together to produce young.

Migration Traveling at regular times of the year in search of food, a suitable climate, or a place to mate and raise young.

Molt To shed a coat of fur or feathers and to grow another.

Nurse To drink milk from a mother's body.

Oxygen The part of the air we breathe that is used by the body.

Pack ice Ice formed by the crashing together of chunks of ice.

Pinnipeds A group of animals with feet specially shaped as flippers. Seals, Sea Lions, and walruses are pinnipeds.

Predator An animal that hunts other animals for food.

Pup A young seal.

Pupil The part of the eye that opens and closes to take in light.

Tide pool A pool of water left on shore when the tide goes out.

Index

PHOTO CREDITS
Cover: Kennon Cooke, *Valan Photos.* **Interiors:** *Valan Photos:* Harold V. Green, 4; Val & Alan Wilkinson, 7, 34; Stephen J. Krasemann, 8, 37; François Lepine, 16; W. Hoek, 26; Esther Schmidt, 30; Valan Photos, 40; Anthony J. Bond, 44. /*Ivy Images:* Norman Lightfoot, 11. /Fred Bruemmer, 12, 20, 29, 33, 38-39, 43. /*Thomas Stack & Associates:* Randy Morse, 15. /*Eco-Art Productions:* Norman Lightfoot, 19. /Wayne Lynch, 23.

Getting To Know...

Nature's Children

MICE

Susan Horner
and
Celia B. Lottridge

SCHOLASTIC INC.

New York Toronto London Auckland Sydney
Mexico City New Delhi Hong Kong Buenos Aires

Facts in Brief

Classification of North American mice

    Class: *Mammalis* (mammals)

    Order: *Rodentia* (rodents)

    Family: *Muridae* (rats, mice, and voles)

              Zapodidae (Jumping Mice)

    Genus: 9 genera of mice, 2 of Jumping Mice, and 3 of voles found in North America

    Species: 122 species of mice, Jumping Mice, and voles found in North America

World distribution. The common house mouse originated in Europe and is still found there. Some native North American mice are also found in Central and South America; the rest are exclusive to North America.

Habitat. Varies with species.

Distinctive physical characteristics. Vary with species.

Habits and diet. Vary with species.

Published by Scholastic Inc.
90 Old Sherman Turnpike, Danbury, Connecticut 06816.

SCHOLASTIC and associated logos are trademarks of Scholastic Inc.

ISBN 0-7172-6696-6   Printed in the U.S.A.

Edited by: Elizabeth Grace Zuraw   *Photo Editor:* Nancy Norton
Photo Rights: Ivy Images   *Cover Design*: Niemand Design

Have you ever wondered . . .

Mice probably appear in more stories, nursery rhymes, fables, and cartoons than any other animal. But do all those make-believe mice tell us very much about real mice?

Think for a moment about the Aesop fable in which the Town Mouse invites the Country Mouse to visit him, boasting of his splendid house and the exciting things to do—and eat— in the city. At first the Country Mouse is very impressed by everything, especially all the fancy city food. But he soon learns that city life can also be noisy and dangerous. Before long the Country Mouse packs up and heads back to his own home where he lives much more simply—but in peace.

Just what sort of life was the Country Mouse going back to? What sort of house did it have? What did it eat? And was life in the country really less exciting—and less dangerous—than life in the city? Let's take a closer look at some mice to find out.

Opposite page: *The long sensitive whiskers of the White-footed Mouse enable it to feel objects in the dark.*

Mice Everywhere

Mice are found in many different *habitats,* the types of places animals naturally live in. Field, forest, mountain, attic or cellar, hot or cold climate, wet or dry land—nearly every type of place is home to one or more kinds of mice. Some live in the far north and spend much of their lives in tunnels under the snow. Others live in deserts where they avoid the hot sun by living in *burrows,* holes dug in the ground. There are mice that are excellent swimmers; they live in marshy places. And there are mice that nest in trees and never come down to the ground.

The word *mouse* isn't the name of one particular animal. The word is used to refer to a large group of animals that are closely related because they have sharp teeth for gnawing. In North America alone there are hundreds of kinds of mice. Some live in only one tiny area. The Sitka Mouse, for instance, is found only on the smaller Queen Charlotte Islands off Canada's west coast. Other kinds of mice are found across almost all of the continent.

If Aesop had been writing his story in North America instead of ancient Greece, his Country Mouse probably would have been a Deer Mouse or a Meadow Vole.

Deer Mice are the most widespread of all North American mice. They live about as far north as the tree line in artic regions and all the way south through Central Mexico. But you won't find Deer Mice in Florida or other swampy regions of the South. They prefer reasonably dry places.

Meadow Voles are almost as common as Deer Mice, but they're fussier about the kind of place they live in. They like fairly wet regions and avoid dense forests and dry grasslands.

Probably the best known kind of mouse is the house mouse. It belongs to a separate family of Old World mice that came to the New World as stowaways on ships. Unlike its field- and forest-loving relatives, it most commonly lives where people do. It often nests in houses, garages, warehouses, barns, or other places where people keep food. Aesop's Town Mouse most likely would have been a house mouse.

Opposite page: *The Deer Mouse is sometimes called a "wood mouse" because it often lives in the forest.*

A Mouse by Any Other Name

Mice are *rodents,* animals with very sharp front teeth that are especially good for gnawing. In addition, a rodent's teeth never stop growing.

Mice are distant relatives of beavers, muskrats, porcupines, squirrels, and chipmunks. They're more closely related to lemmings and rats, but the mouse's closest relatives are the *voles.*

You've probably seen a vole, even though you may not have known the animal by its correct name. The most widespread vole of all, the Meadow Vole, is the little scampering creature often seen in barns, farmyards, and fields. But even though it's technically a vole, it is commonly called the field mouse.

It's not surprising that people mix up mice and voles. The two animals are very much alike. So how can we tell who's who? Generally speaking, mice are more slender than voles, their faces are more pointed, their ears and eyes are bigger, and their tails are longer.

Opposite page: *The Meadow Vole is probably the most familiar rodent in North America. The name* rodent *comes from a Latin word that means "to gnaw."*

Mouse

Vole

How to Meet a Mouse

Walk through any field or woods and you'll probably pass very close to any number of mice and voles without even knowing it. But if you actually want to meet a mouse, you must choose your time carefully. Most mice and voles are *nocturnal,* or active mainly at night, so that's when your chances are greatest for spotting one. Beyond that, you'll have to be really patient and sit very still, perhaps for a long time.

Mice are timid creatures, ready to flee at any hint of danger. In most cases, their eyesight is not very good, but they have a keen sense of hearing. The slightest sound you make—a sniff or a crack of a twig or a rustle of leaves—will send a mouse scurrying for cover. With strong legs to help it run fast and jump far, a frightened mouse will be gone before you can even catch a glimpse of it.

Opposite page: *The word* mouse *means "thief" in Sanskrit, an ancient Hindu language. Mice earned that name because even in ancient times, they often stole from people's food supplies.*

Now You See It, Now You Don't

To get a good look at a mouse, there's one more thing you'll need in addition to patience. You must also be very alert. Why? Mice come in a variety of shades and combinations of grays and browns. These colors blend in well with their surroundings and make mice difficult to see. *Camouflage* is the name given to the coloring and markings on an animal that enable it to blend in with its surroundings.

Deer Mice get their name from their coloring, which resembles that of a deer—reddish brown with lighter underparts. But over time, even Deer Mice have developed some variations. Those that live in shadowy woodlands are darker than those that live in the open.

You can tell that this Deer Mouse makes its home in the woods: It has a dark gray coat that blends in with the shadowy forest.

Small as a Mouse

We all know that mice are small. But there's small…and then there's small. The tiniest full-grown North American mouse may be only about 5 inches (13 centimeters) long—and about half of that is its tail! A mouse that size may weigh less than half an ounce (as little as 11 grams). The largest mice are about twice that size.

Even within one *species,* or kind, of mouse, there can be great variations. Deer Mice, for instance, come in a wide range of sizes. The largest Deer Mouse is about twice as big as the smallest mouse of the same species.

It's not much of a mystery how the Red-backed Vole got its name.

Tails That Tell Tales

It's generally true that voles have shorter tails than mice. But just as with the overall size of different mice and voles, there's a great deal of variation in the length of their tails. The Meadow Vole's tail is only about one-third the length of the rest of its body, while the Long-tailed Vole's tail is more than half as long as its body.

And there can be surprisingly big differences within one species. Some kinds of Deer Mice, for instance, have tails that are only about half as long as their bodies, while other Deer Mice have tails that are longer than their bodies. The length of a Deer Mouse's tail can tell you something about how and where it lives. Those with longer tails usually do a lot of tree climbing. They use their longer tails for balance. Shorter-tailed Deer Mice usually live where there are few or no trees.

This mouse is an expert acrobat, thanks to a long tail that helps balance the little animal.

Mice in Motion

Scurry, scamper, scuttle…these are the words we associate with mice on the move. In fact, mice always seem to be in a hurry, dashing here and there and back again on their little, sharply-clawed feet.

Many mice are also good climbers and some are excellent swimmers. A few can even swim across streams. Some mice take to water mainly to escape *predators,* animals that hunt other animals for food. But other mice seem to dive in just for the fun of it.

And most mice can jump. In fact, one family of mice jumps so well that they're called—what else?—Jumping Mice. With extra-long *hind,* or back, legs, the best jumpers among them can leap as far as 3 to 4 yards (almost 3 to 4 meters). That's about 16 times the length of a Jumping Mouse's body from its nose to the tip of its tail. Few human long jumpers can come close to jumping even five times their own height.

A Jumping Mouse is skilled at making a series of zigzagging leaps that help it flee from predators.

Jumping Mouse pawprints

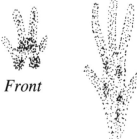

Front

Hind

White-footed Mouse pawprints

Front

Hind

Homebodies

Aesop's Country Mouse didn't seem to mind traveling from his country home to the city. But most mice are not great travelers. Many spend their entire lives dashing to and fro in an area that's probably not much bigger than a backyard. The few kinds of mice that do wander farther afield rarely go more than the length of a city block in any direction from their nest. The area that a mouse regularly travels in is known as its *home range,* and the mouse knows every nook, cranny, dip, and bump in it.

While few mice ever leave their home range, they don't usually mind sharing it. Home ranges of different mice usually overlap without any of the mice getting upset. But when their babies are small, adult mice are very defensive of the area right around their nest.

The Meadow Vole tends to be active both day and night, stopping every now and then to take a short nap.

Mouse Trails

You would think that mice must have a hard time getting around in woods and fields. After all, their little legs may be very strong but they're also very short. The loose layer of fallen leaves and pine needles that usually covers the forest floor would be thigh-deep to most mice, and meadow grasses would loom as tall as giant oaks would to you. So how do mice manage?

Have you ever noticed that if people keep using a shortcut across a lawn or through a field, the grass and plants soon stop growing there? Well, the same principle works for mice. They establish a network of tiny paths, sometimes even with bridges and tunnels, that go from their nests to various useful spots in their home range.

Some mice may be able to beat down a path just by their repeated comings and goings. Others bite off the grasses in their way and then trample down the stubs. And some don't bother doing all this work themselves. They simply use the "highways" built by their relatives.

Opposite page: *Mice can be skillful climbers. This Deer Mouse scampers fearlessly along a tree branch.*

Danger Everywhere

Opposite page: *Mice must always be alert for enemies. Are this little mouse's ears perked up at a sound that could be a nearby house cat or weasel?*

Mouse highways aren't just a lazy mouse's way of making life easier for itself. They serve a useful purpose. Mice have to be able to move quickly and they need a clear, easy way to dash back to their nest. Why? Because mice are prey to a great variety and number of enemies. *Prey* is an animal hunted by another animal for food.

Animals that hunt mice include coyotes, foxes, weasels, skunks, raccoons, bears, shrews, house cats, squirrels, some snakes, turtles, fish, and birds of prey. The list changes a bit with the kind of mouse and its habits. For example, mice that are active at night need not worry about hawks or eagles, birds that hunt by day. And mice that stay away from water have no fish enemies. But it's safe to say that any animal that eats meat sees a mouse as a tasty dinner.

This may seem unfair to mice, but it's all part of the balance of nature. If all mice lived and had babies, there'd soon be so many mice that plants would disappear. Mice would eat them all. At the same time, if there weren't so many mice, many animals would starve.

Mouse Menus

Like many wild animals, mice spend most of their waking hours searching for food and eating it. In general, mice aren't fussy eaters. They eat whatever is available—and they eat a lot of it. This doesn't mean that different kinds of mice don't have their favorite foods. Deer Mice prefer seeds, but they'll also nibble on buds and tender green leaves in the spring. Meadow Voles are mainly grass eaters, but when grass runs out, they'll make do with seeds, roots, and even twig bark.

Almost all mice enjoy an occasional tasty meat snack, such as a caterpillar, cutworm, or spider. And one mouse, the Northern Grasshopper Mouse, eats mainly insects. Even though it will eat almost any insect or insect egg, its favorite is—you guessed it— grasshoppers.

House mice eat nearly anything people eat, as well as insects and any other meat or plant matter that's available. They also eat such household items as leather and soap.

Opposite page: *For creatures that never stray far from home, mice certainly get around. This mouse isn't afraid to go out on a limb in search of a snack!*

Clean and Tidy

Would it surprise you to learn that mice and cats have something in common? Actually, it's something they share with many animals— they like to keep clean.

A mouse sits up on its haunches to *groom,* or clean, itself, using its tail for extra support. It washes its face with its forepaws, carefully rubbing its ears. Then it strokes down its back and its belly, combing the fur with its tiny claws. Finally, it uses its teeth and tongue to groom its feet and tail.

Mice also like to live in clean homes, and many establish special toilet areas away from their nest. Many mice live in *colonies,* or groups, and those that do often set up community toilets, and share the work of building the paths that lead to them.

Some mice, such as Deer Mice, don't bother building toilets. They seem to find it easier to build a new nest when the old one gets too dirty.

Opposite page: A White-footed Mouse grooms itself by licking its front paws.

Mouse Houses

Adult mice usually each have their own home nest, at least for most of the year. This is true of mice that live in colonies, too.

Mouse houses come in many sizes. Most are ball shaped and made of grasses and twigs and anything else that's handy: bits of bone, cloth, fur, string, paper—whatever odds and ends the builder happens to find. The inside of a mouse house is hollow and lined with soft material such as moss, cattail fuzz, or the feathery down of dandelions or thistle.

Mice build their nests almost anywhere that is protected enough for the owner to feel safe. Some mice hide their nests in underground burrows they dig themselves, while some borrow burrows abandoned by other animals. Other favorite hiding places are under logs and rocks, in tree hollows or stumps, and in clumps of grass or weeds. Mice have even been known to take over deserted birds' nests.

House mice may build nests in the dark warm corners of houses, attics, garages, or barns, but some live in woodland burrows.

Opposite page: *This Deer Mouse has made a home in a hollow log.*

Mice in Winter

Much like people, mice have various ways of coping with winter's cold and snow.

Jumping Mice *hibernate,* or go into a deep sleep until spring. They also eat a lot in the fall to put on a layer of fat. The extra fat provides what little energy their bodies need while they're hibernating.

This is how a Jumping Mouse hibernates. Its tail is curled up around its body.

Most mice and voles, however, remain active all winter—though some more than others. Many kinds of mice have stretchy cheek pouches in which they collect seeds. In the fall they gather as many seeds as they can and hide them in storage chambers near their nest. As long as their stored supply lasts, they only have to make very short trips to the storage places.

These mice spend the rest of their time huddled together for warmth in groups of 10 to 15. Among White-footed Mice, there's a definite "pecking order" in the group. One mouse quickly establishes itself as top mouse and gets the warmest spot in the middle. The least aggressive members of the group end up on the colder edges.

A White-footed Mouse pokes its nose out of its burrow.

Business as Usual

Most voles don't collect very much extra food in the fall. For that reason, they're almost as active during the winter as they are in summer.

Those that live mainly underground travel back and forth through their tunnels as usual. Meadow Voles and others tunnel through the snow to use the same surface runways they use in summer.

Opposite page: *Because food is harder to find in winter, this vole will have to work harder than it does in summer to find enough to eat.*

Mice and voles use tunnels under the snow to get around during the winter.

Squeal, Chatter, Cheep

You'd have a tough time eavesdropping on a mouse "conversation." Some mice hardly ever make sounds, and even the more vocal ones have very soft, tiny voices.

Those soft voices, however, can make a surprising variety of sounds. Most mice squeak and squeal, and many chirp and chatter as well. A few whistle in a way that sounds rather like an insect's hum. One vole, the Singing Vole, is even named for its high-pitched, throbbing call. And believe it or not, the Northern Grasshopper Mouse sometimes sits on its haunches, throws back its head, and howls like a miniature coyote!

Some mice have special sounds they make in certain situations. For instance, many thump when they're alarmed—some with their front paws, others with their tail. And some female mice have a special squeak that lets males know they're ready to *mate,* or come together, to produce young.

Starting a Family

When mice are ready to mate—which is several times a year—the male and female share a nest for a few days. They will spend these days grooming each other and playfully chasing each other around the area near the nest.

Depending on the kind of mouse, the male may leave after mating or he may stay nearby and help care for the babies after they're born. Either way, the mother prepares the nursery by herself. She either relines her nest with the softest material she can find or builds a brand new one.

These newborn Deer Mice are cozy in the fluffy nest that their mother made for them from a soft cottony material.

Big Families

Mouse babies are born about three weeks after their parents mate. There are usually five to seven babies in a *litter*—the animals that are born together—but sometimes many more are born. The number depends on the species of mouse, the age of the mother, and how well she has been eating.

Newborn mice are tiny—1.5 inches (less than 4 centimeters) long, including their tails. That's shorter than most erasers! The babies are born blind, deaf, and with no hair except for tiny whiskers.

Fast-growing Babies

Baby mice grow amazingly fast. For the first two days of their life, their mother doesn't leave the nest so that the babies can almost continually *nurse,* or drink milk from her body. The babies' skin is so transparent that you'd actually be able to see the milk flowing into them as they feed!

A new family of White-footed Mice feeds on its mother's milk.

Within four days, however, the babies have a little fur, and in one week, they've doubled their birth weight. By two weeks, their eyes have opened so that they can see and are able to move around. They're still nursing but they can also eat berries and seeds.

Mice, especially Deer Mice, are caring mothers. If the nest is disturbed, a Deer Mouse mother will move her babies to a safer place. Each baby stays with her by holding on tight to one of her *teats,* the part of the mother's body through which a baby drinks her milk. If a baby should fall off, the mother gently picks it up in her mouth by the scruff of its neck and carries it to the new nest.

If the father is still around, he helps keep the babies clean and helps them stay warm by cuddling up to them. He also repairs the nest and will go after any baby that strays, bringing it back home. Once the babies are old enough, he takes them on food-finding expeditions.

Opposite page: *Though they have large eyes, mice can't see very well. Even if people were close by, this mouse wouldn't know it—unless the people made a sound, which the mouse's keen ears would quickly pick up.*

Mice Forever

By the time they're a few weeks old, most mice are grown up and ready to fend for themselves. And by the time they're three or four months old, they're ready to start their own families. If a mouse is lucky and manages to avoid predators, it can expect to live about a year and a half.

Few animals have learned to adapt to as many different conditions as mice, and few reproduce as rapidly. Even though their lives are short and hurried, you can be quite sure that the next time you walk through a nearby field or woods, some little mouse or vole will be scampering about or snoozing in its nest.

So be sure to stop for a few minutes. Sit very still and watch carefully. With a little bit of luck, your patience may be rewarded with a glimpse of one of these fascinating little creatures.

Words To Know

Burrow   A hole dug in the ground by an animal for use as a home.

Camouflage   Coloring and markings on an animal that help it blend in with its surroundings.

Colony   A group of animals that live together.

Groom   To brush and clean hair or fur.

Habitat   The type of area an animal or plant naturally lives in.

Hibernate   To go into a kind of heavy sleep for the winter. When animals hibernate, their breathing and heart rate slow, and their body temperature drops.

Home range   The area that a mouse regularly travels and lives in.

Hind   Situated at the back of an animal's body.

Litter   The young animals that are born together.

Mate   To come together to produce young.

Teat   The part of a mother's body through which a baby drinks her milk.

Nocturnal   Active mainly at night.

Nurse   To drink milk from a mother's body.

Predator   An animal that hunts other animals for food.

Prey   An animal hunted by another animal for food. A bird that hunts animals for food is often called a bird of prey.

Rodent   An animal with sharp teeth that are especially good for gnawing.

Species   A class or kind of animal that has certain traits in common.

Tundra   Flat, treeless land in Arctic regions.

Vole   A very close relative of the mouse.

Index

PHOTO CREDITS

Cover: Bill Ivy. **Interiors:** *Valan Photos:* Robert C. Simpson, 4, 23; J. R. Page, 7, 39; Duane Sept, 16; Michel Quintin, 19, 24; François Morneau, 20; Albert Kuhnigk, 27; Francis Lepine, 28; Dennis Schmidt, 32; John Fowler, 40. /Bill Ivy, 8, 11, 12, 15, 36, 44. /*Ivy Images:* Robert McCaw, 31, 35; Bill Beatty, 43.

Brilliant
BEADING

15 stylish step-by-step projects

Anna Morgan

NEW
HOLLAND

Published in 2005 by
New Holland Publishers (UK) Ltd
London · Cape Town · Sydney · Auckland

Garfield House
86–88 Edgware Road
London
W2 2EA
United Kingdom
www.newhollandpublishers.com

80 McKenzie Street
Cape Town 8001
South Africa

14 Aquatic Drive
Frenchs Forest, NSW 2086
Australia

218 Lake Road
Northcote, Auckland
New Zealand

ISBN 1 84330 987 4

Senior Editor: Clare Hubbard
Photographer: Shona Wood
Design: Peter Crump
Template Illustrations: Stephen Dew
Production: Ben Byram-Wigfield
Editorial Direction: Rosemary Wilkinson

1 3 5 7 9 10 8 6 4 2

Reproduction by Pica Digital Pte., Singapore
Printed and bound by Times Offset (M) Sdn. Bhd., Malaysia

Note
The author and publishers have made every effort to
ensure that all instructions given in this book are safe and
accurate, but they cannot accept liability for any resulting
injury or loss or damage to either property or person,
whether direct or consequential and howsoever arising.

CONTENTS

PROJECTS

Introduction

Beading has never been more popular. Department and designer stores are full of beautiful beaded items – sumptuous throws, cushions, glittering lampshades, lanterns, candle surrounds – all have their place in the contemporary home. However, it is so much more satisfying to make the items yourself, with beads you've chosen, and colours that will complement your personal spaces, tailor-made to suit your taste and add beauty, interest and sparkle to your home.

From earliest times, people have adorned themselves with "beads", primarily in the form of berries, seeds, stones and shells. Later, beads came to be manufactured from clay, glass, metal and crystals and, more recently, acrylics and plastics. There is something irresistible about beads. It's a combination of their berry-like size, their glossy or sparkling surfaces and the array of sumptuous colours and myriad designs. They are confectionery for the eyes. It is no wonder that we want them, not only to decorate our person, but around us, to gaze at whilst we relax within our own home.

Many people collect beads, keeping broken necklaces with the thought that one day they'll do something with them. Well wait no longer and get them out! Now is the perfect time to wash off the dust and get started. Look through the book for a suitable project to begin with. There are many ways in which you can enhance your home using beads. In this book there are 15 projects designed to suit both beginners and more experienced crafters. Four basic techniques are used – sewing beads directly onto fabric, making beaded fringes with needle and cotton, threading beads onto wire to form structures, and mixing beads with a glue medium to form encrusted surfaces. There are clear step-by-step instructions that will not only enable you to follow a project through, but will give you enough information to start designing your own. Start thinking about colourways or using different types of beads.

All the materials used within this book are easily available; beading and tapestry needles from good needlework stores, wires from hardware or gardening suppliers. If you don't have a local bead supplier, use those listed on page 95. Many of them offer online shopping or mail-order. I have used a range of beads, from the ubiquitous rocailles or seed beads to Chinese porcelain, recycled Ghanaian glass and sparkling Austrian crystal beads. Buying beads can be expensive, however, so if cost is an issue use beads from discarded necklaces or hunt in charity shops and flea markets – many attractive gems can be found in this way.

Some of the projects in this book lend themselves to special occasions. For example, the table runner, wine glass charmers and coathanger have a nuptial feel. Weddings are occasions when you can go to town with decoration, lavishing time and expense to add glow and glitter to the special day, and beading certainly does this. But these projects don't have to be exclusively for weddings – with a change of emphasis and colour, they can all be adapted to suit other occasions.

Once you've got the "bug" for beading, there is no end to what can be achieved, not only to create beautiful accessories for your own home, but also gifts for others. How special to give a present that has been hand-beaded by you for a close friend or relative.

Getting started

The materials and equipment used in the projects are readily available from craft, needlework and hardware shops.

MATERIALS

Scissors

These are purely for cutting fabric, ribbon and tape – don't attempt to cut wire with them, always use wire cutters.

Beading needles

These are extremely thin, bendy needles. If you are threading up strings of beads it is best to use a long one. If you are stitching on individual beads choose a short needle, they are more manageable.

Tapestry needles

These have large eyes that are big enough to thread thin ribbons through (see Silk tassel, pages 28–31). Choose needles with thin shanks.

Silver thread

Decorative threads are very effective in beading projects. Silver thread has been used to make the butterflies' antennae on the Butterfly cushion (see pages 78–83).

Cotton thread and beeswax

All of the sewing projects in this book have been made using ordinary cottons. Because beading needles are very hard to thread, it can help if you use beeswax and wax the end of the thread – this binds the filaments together into a point.

Silk ribbon

This is available in a wide range of colours and complements beads. It can be used to trim lampshades and cushions, beads can be directly sewn onto the ribbon or suspended from it in a fringe.

Pencils

A propelling pencil is useful for marking through templates – the point is fine and hard enough to pierce the paper without ripping it, leaving a fine mark. If you don't have one, be sure to sharpen an ordinary pencil to a fine point.

Pins

These are needed when you are stitching beaded fringes onto items and can be useful for marking measurements.

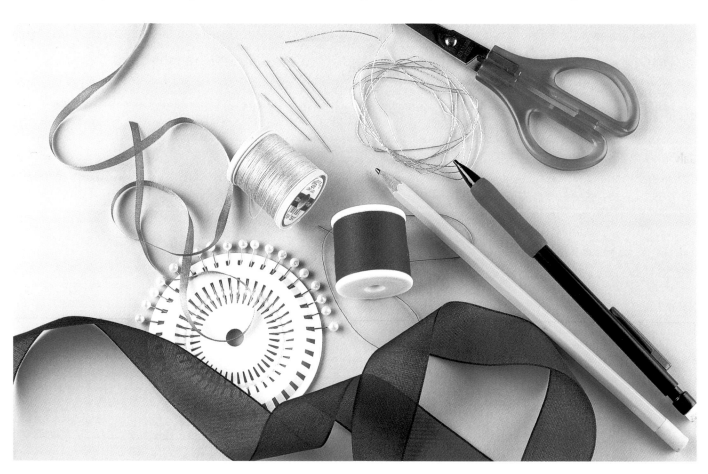

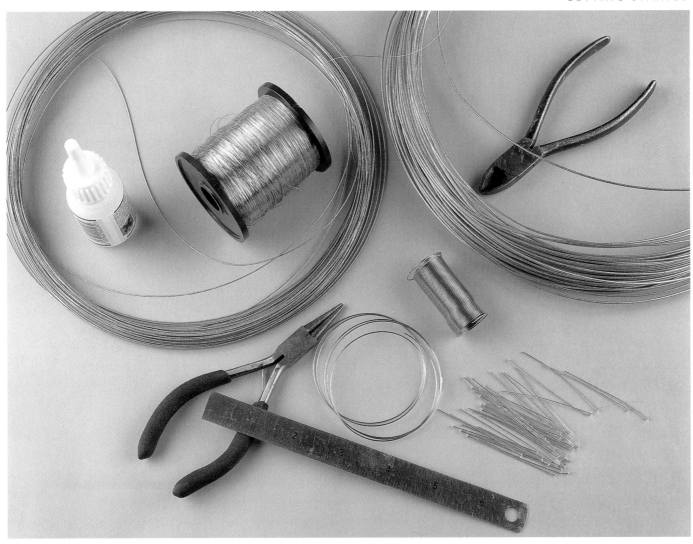

EQUIPMENT

Galvanized wire

Ordinary galvanized garden wire has been used for the majority of projects in this book. It is readily available from hardware shops in a wide range of widths. The projects in this book use 1.6 mm and 0.8 mm.

Florist's wire

This is fine wire, good for binding, and was used for the Candle ring (see pages 88–93). It can be purchased from florists, gardening shops and some hardware stores.

Superglue

Useful for glueing on beads or spacing them out along wire – choose one that is suitable for use with both wire and glass. Use according to the manufacturer's instructions.

Jewellery pliers

These are small, round-nosed tools, good for shaping wire and forming spirals, loops, and hooks and eyes for joining wire.

Ruler

It is important to use a ruler to achieve an even spacing when making fringes, otherwise they end up looking messy.

Memory wire

This is sprung wire, and it comes in coils. If pulled or pressed it will revert back to its original shape. It is possible to distort it forcibly with pressure. The bracelet size was used for the Wine glass charmers (see pages 46–50). The wire had to be reshaped to fit around the stem. The ring size was used to make the Stem glass charmers on page 50.

Head pins

These are generally used for jewellery-making, particularly earrings. They are bendy wires with a head that will hold a bead on. They have been used in this book in the Flower bouquet (see pages 41–45).

Wire cutters

Very useful for beading projects involving wirework. If you don't have a pair, consider your pliers. Many have a wire cutting edge on the side.

BEAD TYPES

A trip to the bead shop is both exciting and overwhelming as there are so many types to choose from. Here's a guide to help you with your selection.

Rocailles

Rocailles, literally "seeds", are little round beads. They are available in different sizes: 11/0 are usually the smallest and 5/0 about the largest. They come in a variety of different colours and finishes.

Bugles

These are thin, rod-like beads. There are not as many different types and finishes as rocailles, but the range available is fairly comprehensive.

Delicas and Z-cut beads

These are good for weaving and embroidery.

1. Opaque glass, size 10/0

2. Frosted transparent glass, size 6/0

3. Transparent rainbow, sizes 8/0 and 6/0 (sometimes known as "bubbly finish")

4. Iridescent (sometimes known as "oily finish"), size 6/0

5. Colour-lined (these are translucent coloured glass beads with a different coloured lining which gives a two-tone effect), size 6/0

6. Silver-lined (these are translucent colours with a silver lining which makes them extra shiny)

7. Frosted silver-lined, sizes 6/0 and 8/0

8. Matt striped, size 11/0

9. Opaque pearlized, size 8/0

10. Colour-lined Z-cut delicas (faceted beads)

11. Silver-lined bugles

12. Variegated frosted bugles

13. Frosted translucent rocailles with off-centre holes

14. Silver-lined rocailles with off-centre holes

15. Metallic finish rocailles, size 11/0

16. Silver delicas

17. Transparent sausage glass beads

18. Cat's eye cubes

19. Round glass beads

20. Glass beads with raised spots

21. Synthetic pearls – these are available in more shapes and colours than you may think

22. Frosted foil-lined beads

23. Miracle beads (have an extraordinarily shiny finish)

24. Ghanaian recycled glass beads (handmade)

25. Foiled lamp beads – foils lie underneath the glass to give a really luscious finish

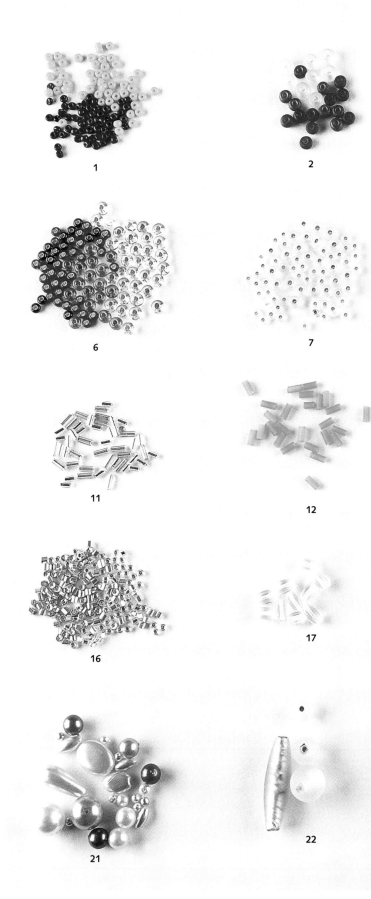

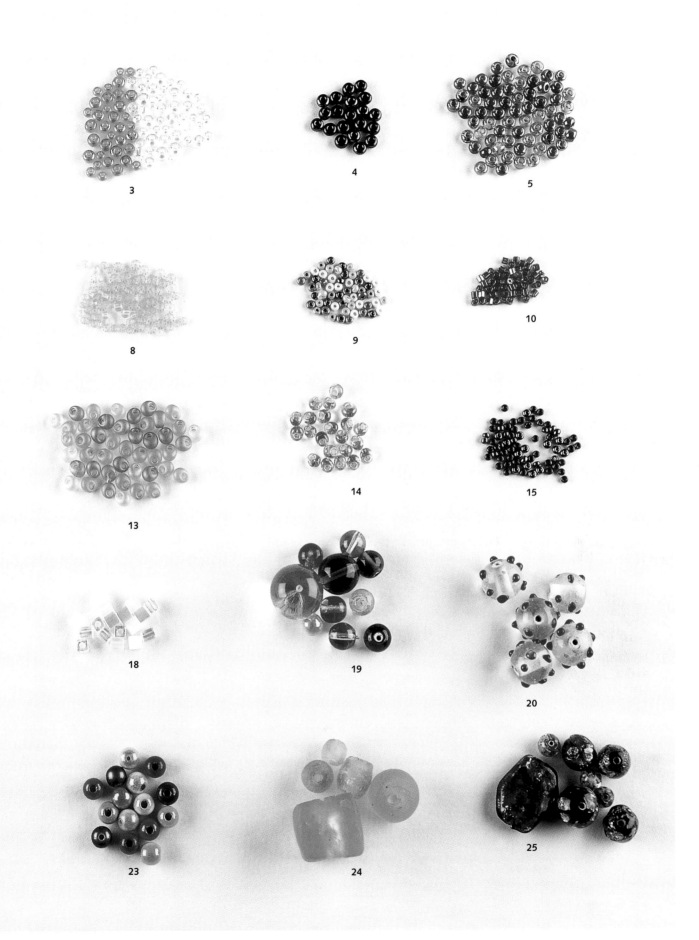

3

4

5

8

9

10

13

14

15

18

19

20

23

24

25

BEAD SHAPES AND FINISHES

Beads are available in myriad shapes and finishes. This is just a selection of what's available. If your local supplier does not stock what you want, try a mail-order supplier.

1. Transparent glass drops
2. Frosted lustre-finished drops
3. Dagger drops
4. Lustre dagger drops
5. Fire-polished faceted drops
6. Leaves (various)
7. Flowers (various)
8. Hearts (various)
9. Stars (various)
10. Cat's eye beads (various shapes)
11. Cones (frosted glass/ridged silver lined) etc.
12. Pearl oats
13. Flat diamonds (lustre finish)
14. Top-drilled drops (lustre finish)
15. Pearl drops
16. Frosted glass triangles (top-drilled)
17. Potato beads 6 x 8 mm (¼ x ⅜ in) and 4 x 6 mm (⅛ x ¼ in)
18. Lustre-finished beads (various shapes)
19. Transparent faceted bi-cones
20. Flat oval pearls
21. Frosted glass beads
22. Porcelain character beads
23. Colour-lined frosted triangular beads (centre-drilled)
24. Oval foil-lined beads
25. Sunburst
26. Flat disc beads
27. Faceted glass beads
28. Indian lozenge beads

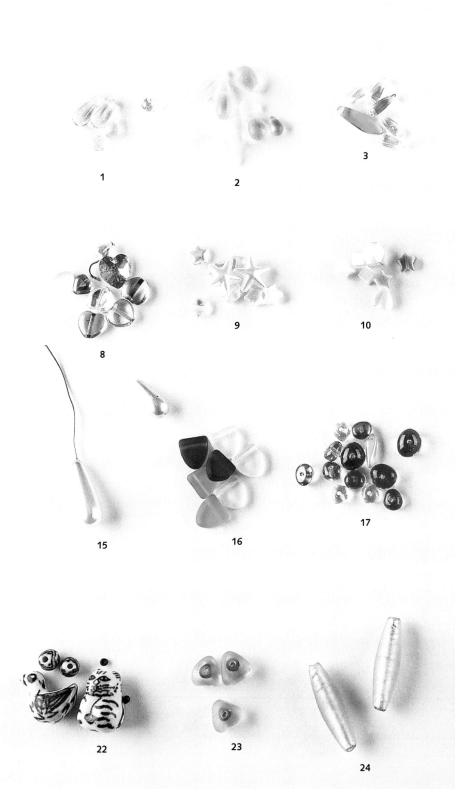

4

5

6

7

11

12

13

14

18

19

20

21

25

26

27

28

Basic techniques

Encrusting

This is achieved by mixing beads with P.V.A (craft glue). The mix can then be used to decorate a surface, giving it a fantastic grotto-like texture. Use waterproof P.V.A. if your item is likely to get wet or will be exposed to steam. Once dry, the P.V.A. becomes transparent, leaving the beads held in position.

1 Mix the beads with the P.V.A. Make sure the mixture isn't too wet – you need just enough P.V.A. to bind the beads.

2 Make sure the surface to be treated is lying flat, then spoon the mixture on. Spread it with a knife or similar implement. If you want a greater depth in some areas than others, encrust to 1 cm (½ in) depth at a time, leaving to dry in between layers, and build up the surface as required.

Glueing

Spacing If you want beads spaced out along a wire, one way to achieve this is to use superglue. Dab the glue onto the wire, then slide the bead onto the glue with a pin or similar implement (take care not to get glue on your hands). This technique is often used for necklaces. It gives a very light, lacy, delicate effect.

Finishing If you want a smooth line of wired beads, like the Flower bouquet (see pages 41–45), you can glue on the last bead. This saves twisting loops in the wire and looks neater.

Suspending beads using jewellery head pins

A head pin is a long, bendable pin used mainly in jewellery-making. The head acts as a stopper to keep the bead from falling off.

1 Thread your beads onto the pin. If your main bead has a bigger hole than the head, you will need to use a smaller bead first, like this seed pearl.

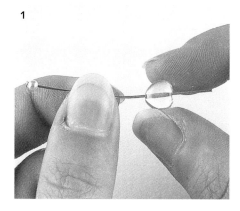

2 Once your beads are threaded on, allow 1 cm (½ in) of wire to protrude. Snip off any excess. Form the wire into a small loop with your jewellery pliers. Don't close the loop until you have hung the pin in position.

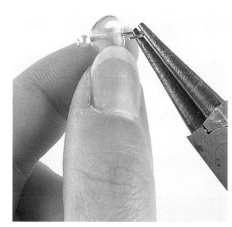

Suspending beads using wire

1 Cut a length of 0.8 mm galvanized wire or similar. Thread on a droplet bead and bend 1 cm (½ in) of wire back. Squeeze the double wire together at the top of the bead and thread on other beads. (You will need beads with a large enough hole to take the doubled thickness of wire.)

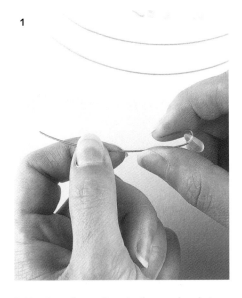

2 Use jewellery pliers to form a hook (see step 2, Suspending beads using jewellery head pins, opposite), then suspend and close up the gap.

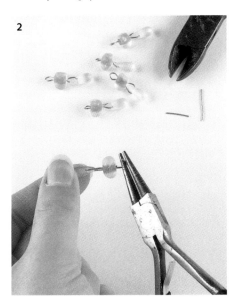

Making a wire loop

Cut a length of wire with wire cutters. Use the round, pointed ends of jewellery pliers to twist the wire into a loop.

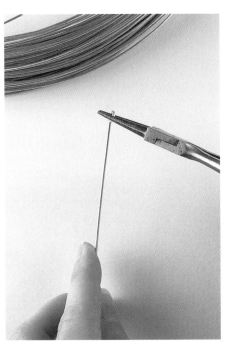

Making an open spiral

Create a loop at the end of a length of wire. Hold the loop of wire firmly with your jewellery pliers and bend the wire round in a spiral, bracing the length of wire against your finger.

Joining wire ends

This technique can be used to join the ends of one piece of wire to form a circle, or to join two pieces of wire together. Use jewellery pliers to create an eye at one end of the wire. Make sure it is a completely closed loop. At the other end, form an open loop (like a hook) at right angles to the eye. Interlock, then use your pliers to close up the loop to secure the join.

Making a tassel

This tassel is used on the Silk cushion (see pages 84–87).

1 Using a beading needle with doubled thread, knot the thread ends together and thread through a colour-lined

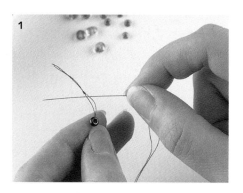

purple/blue rocaille, then insert the needle in between the threads as shown. This will secure the bead.

2 Thread on the head beads that will make the body of the tassel – a green lozenge bead and a flower bead.

3 Use the beading needle to thread on Z-cut delicas. Thread on enough to make a strand 4 cm (1½ in) long.

4 To add weight and beauty to the strand, add an amethyst potato bead, followed by a colour-lined purple/blue rocaille. This will act as a stopper.

5 Next thread the needle back up through the beads and around the colour-lined rocaille at the top. Then insert the needle back through the head beads and repeat steps 3 and 4 to create another strand. Continue until you have as many strands as you need. (The size of the holes in your head beads will dictate how many times you can keep threading through them.) The tassels on the Silk cushion have three strands.

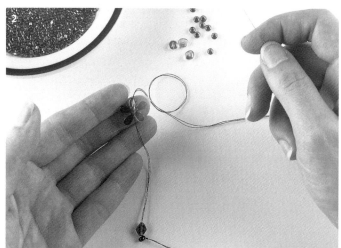

Sewing on beads

1 Use doubled thread if the hole in your bead will permit. Knot the thread and stitch through from the back of the material. Use the point of your needle to pick up the beads and thread them on. When you have enough beads, stitch back through your fabric. Avoid working with too long a length of beads at a time before stitching through. (This will lessen the necessary repair work if the thread breaks at some point.)

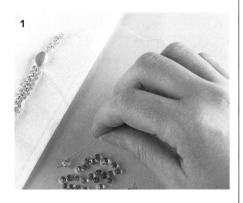

2 You will need to secure these strands of beads to your fabric by couching them. To do this, stitch through the material from the back with a knotted thread (a single strand will do). Then, make a tiny stitch over the beads (actually the gap between each bead) and through to the back. This will hold the beaded thread down securely. You can do this between every bead or every few beads, depending on how much time you have. Make sure you keep your stitches tight in between the beads. They should not be visible from the front.

Fringing

1 Choose beads that will either complement or contrast with the item. Arrange the beads in the sequence you desire. (It sometimes helps to use a strip of double-sided tape to stop the beads rolling around.) If you are not sewing the beads directly onto the item, use ribbon or tape instead. Decide how far apart you want the individual strands to be. Measure the distance between the top beads and mark the intervals with pins.

2 Choose cotton to match the tape or ribbon. Knot the end of the cotton thread and either make a tiny running stitch or overstitch along the edge so that the thread is hardly visible. When you reach the first marked point, thread on your sequence of beads. (Here, I have alternated the sequence.) Use a seed bead at the bottom and thread through it, then back through the beads to the ribbon. Continue to stitch until you reach the next marked position, and so on until you finish your length of fringing. This can then be stitched or glued onto your item.

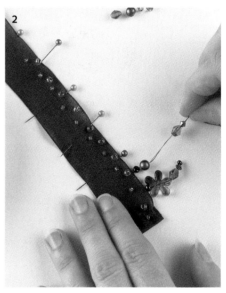

 PROJECTS – step close-ups

Important details are shown in close-up throughout the projects. These are identified by the magnifying glass icon.

Projects

1 page 20

2 page 24

6 page 41

7 page 46

11 page 68

12 page 73

Crystalline frame

An ordinary white wooden frame has been transformed, with a crystalline beaded mixture, into a beautiful item suitable for displaying a wedding photo. (If you can't find a suitable white frame, paint a wooden frame with white primer paint and leave to dry. Then, paint it white or an appropriate colour if you are using different beads to those listed.)

The encrusted effect is easily achieved by mixing a medley of beads with P.V.A. and applying this mixture to the frame. The same technique can be used for encrusting boxes, special books and cards. The materials listed are for a frame measuring approximately 20 x 25 cm (7¾ x 9¾ in).

YOU WILL NEED

Newspaper or scrap paper

P.V.A. (craft glue)

White wooden frame with flat moulding

Bowl

Dessertspoon

Knife or spatula

BEADS

60 sunburst beads

1 vial transparent rocailles size 6/0

1 vial frosted silver-lined rocailles size 6/0

2 vials oily (rainbow-finished clear beads) size 6/0

2 vials oily (rainbow-finished clear beads) size 8/0

1 vial silver-lined bugles size 1'''

1 vial silver-lined rocailles size 8/0

1 vial transparent rocailles size 8/0

1 Cover your work surface with newspaper or scrap paper. Dip the reverse of the sunburst beads in the P.V.A., then position them all around the edge of the frame.

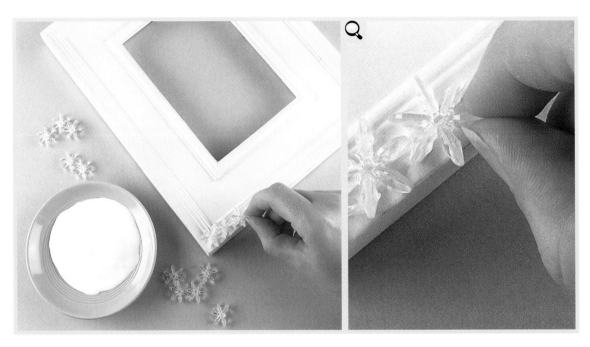

2 Mix together all of the larger seed beads in a bowl, add a couple of dessertspoonfuls of P.V.A. and mix so that the beads bind together.

3 Spoon this mixture around the outer edge of the inner frame and spread out with a knife. Leave to dry.

4 Mix up the smaller beads to a similar consistency with P.V.A., then spoon on and spread around the inner frame. Leave to dry.

Alternative design

This frame has been lined with flat, turquoise triangular beads around its outer edge, and blue/purple colour-lined rocailles on the inside edge. The crystalline beads in between are the same mixture as used for the main project.

ARTIST'S TIP

When trying out your own designs and colourways, test out a small amount of bead mixture on a piece of appropriate coloured paper to see how it will look.

Blue and white bowl cover

Antique or second-hand lace doilies can be purchased inexpensively from charity shops or flea markets. They make very pretty bowl covers, which are particularly useful if you are eating outdoors in summer. The beads not only make them interestingly novel, but act as weights to hold the doily in place over the food. Blue and white is a popular choice for kitchenware, and these little porcelain character beads would complement your china perfectly.

The lace doily used in this project measures 31 cm (12 in) in diameter.

YOU WILL NEED

1 lace doily

Navy blue cotton thread

Beading needle

Scissors

BEADS

1 vial variegated blue frosted rocailles size 6/0

1 vial navy blue rocailles size 8/0

20 porcelain blue and white duck beads

20 porcelain navy blue round beads 5 mm (¼ in)

1 Stitch variegated blue frosted rocailles around the inner
edge of your lace doily to make an attractive inner border.

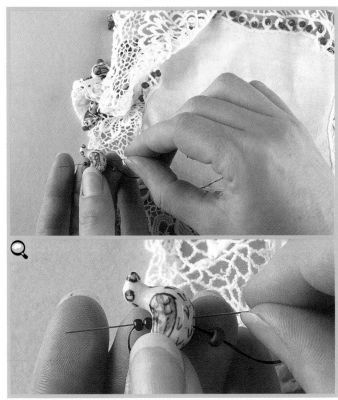

2 Work out the intervals for the beads around your doily (it
helps to have a scalloped edge). The duck beads dangle
alternately with the round porcelain beads. Start with the ducks.
Make a small stitch to attach the thread, then thread on a
couple of navy blue rocailles before the duck.

3 Use a variegated blue frosted rocaille after the duck. This
will hold the beads on. Thread your needle through this,
position it sideways, then pass the needle back through the
duck and rocailles to the doily. Stitch several times onto the lace
to secure and cut off the thread.

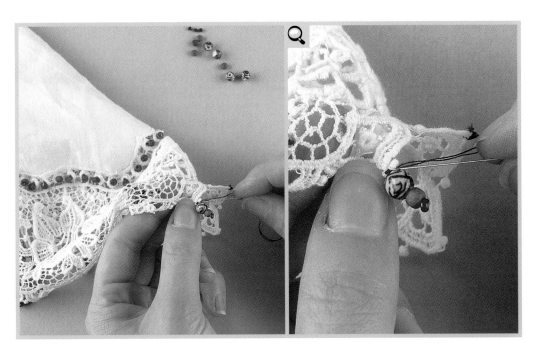

4 Alternate duck bead strands with round porcelain bead strands. To make these, stitch through the doily to attach the thread. Then thread the needle through the porcelain bead and a variegated bead, then a navy blue rocaille and back again, through the variegated and porcelain beads to the doily. Secure with a few stitches and cut off the thread.

Alternative design

These pretty Chinese porcelain beads are available in many different animal shapes. These cats are particularly nice and could be used on a doily to cover a bowl of cream. Glass crystal beads could also be used on a doily for a more sumptuous effect.

Silk tassel

Silk ribbons are available in a sumptuous array of colours and combine beautifully with beads to make these lovely tassels. Tassels can be used on light pulls, curtain tie backs and key rings to add an individual touch to an everyday item. Choose ribbons and beads in colours that will suit your décor. This is where you can really have fun choosing beautiful colours, shapes and textures. (Make sure you choose beads with a large enough hole for the ribbon to pass through.)

YOU WILL NEED

6 m (6 yd) lavender silk ribbon

Ruler

Scissors

Tapestry needle (big eye, slender shaft)

50 cm (20 in) pink silk ribbon

BEADS

50 pink and amethyst round beads 4 mm (⅛ in)

50 pink and amethyst potato beads 6 x 8 mm (¼ x ⅜ in)

100 clear Indian lozenge glass beads 10 x 6 mm (½ x ¼ in)

2 clear round beads 15 mm (⅝ in)

Frosted disc bead 2.5 cm (1 in) diameter

1 pink glass bead 6 mm (¼ in)

1 purple miracle bead 6 mm (¼ in)

1 mauve oval lamp bead 23 x 6 mm (1 x ¼ in)

1 frosted lamp bead

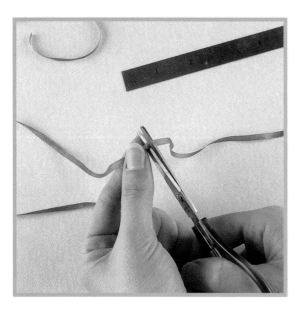

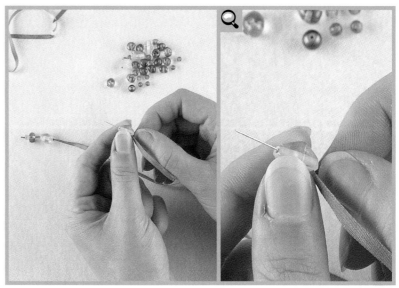

1 Cut the following lengths of lavender ribbon: 10 pieces 25.5 cm (10 in) long, 10 pieces 19 cm (9½ in) long and 5 pieces 11.5 cm (6½ in) long.

2 Thread a piece of ribbon onto the tapestry needle. Tie a knot at the end of the ribbon and thread on the following sequence of beads: a small round bead, a potato bead, a clear lozenge bead, then the same beads in reverse order.

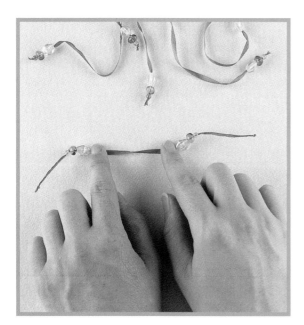

3 Remove the needle and knot the ribbon at the end. Separate the beads and push each group to their respective ends. Repeat on all of the other 24 lengths of ribbon.

4 Group all of the beaded ribbons together. Thread the pink ribbon through the needle and knot both ends together. Wrap the pink ribbon around the middle of the bunch of beaded lavender ribbons, threading the needle through the loop.

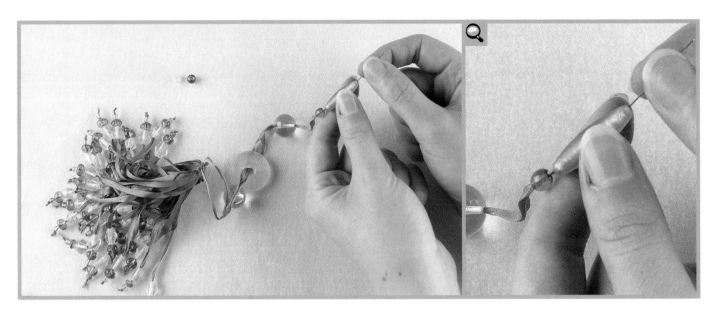

5 Pull the bunch tightly together. Pick up the bunch and arrange so that the knot is on the inside. Then, thread the following onto the pink ribbon in this order: a clear round bead, a frosted disc bead, a clear round bead, a pink glass bead or a purple miracle bead, a mauve oval lamp bead, a purple miracle bead or a pink glass bead and a frosted lamp bead. Cut off the needle. Trim the length of doubled ribbon so that it is long enough to hang the tassel with, and knot the ends.

Alternative design

For a fresher look, choose spring green ribbon. Here, I have used Indian lozenge-shaped beads, colour-lined rocailles, a frosted disc bead, a silver metal bead and recycled Ghanaian glass bead. The more beads you use the heavier the tassel will be, so you may need a stronger cord/ribbon to hang it from.

Fringed lampshade

Jazz up a tired old lampshade with a snazzy beaded fringe. Use a tape edging in a colour that will coordinate with or complement the colour of your shade and beads. Once the beads have been stitched onto the tape, it can be attached to the shade by using double-sided tape or a glue gun. Alternatively, the beads could be directly hung from the shade – either way, it's simple! The quantities of materials suggested are for a shade with a 52.5 cm (20½ in) base circumference.

YOU WILL NEED

Pale blue lampshade

86 cm (34 in) lilac bias binding

Ruler

Scissors

Pencil

Beading needle

Lilac cotton thread

Double-sided carpet tape

BEADS

40 frosted glass lamp beads

20 pink glass beads 6 mm (¼ in)

20 amethyst glass beads 6 mm (¼ in)

1 vial colour-lined blue/purple rocailles size 6/0

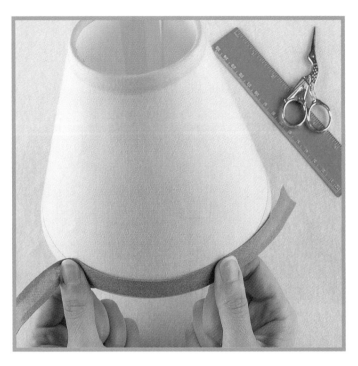

1 Cut a piece of bias binding to fit around the base, allowing 5 mm (¼ in) overlap. Cut a second length to fit around the top rim of the shade, with the same overlap.

2 Mark off 1 cm (½ in) intervals along the length of the bias binding for the base of the shade, allowing for the overlapping tape.

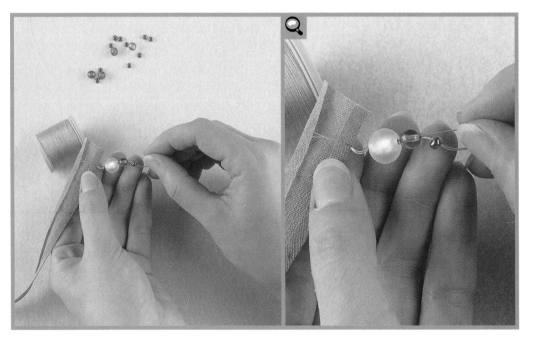

3 Double overstitch at the edge of the tape at the first point where you will be attaching the beads. Then, thread your beading needle through the beads in the following order: a frosted glass lamp bead, a pink or amethyst glass bead (alternate) and a rocaille bead on the end to hold the others in place. Once you have threaded on this final bead, take your needle back up around this bead and through the other beads to the tape.

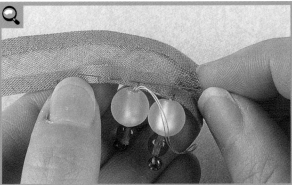

4 Between each set of hanging beads, make little stitches within the groove of the folded edge of bias tape (so that it will not show once the tape is attached), until you reach the next place to attach beads. Remember to alternate the colour of the glass beads to make the effect more interesting.

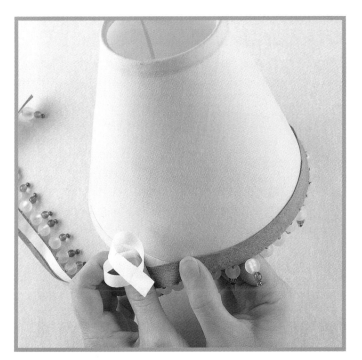

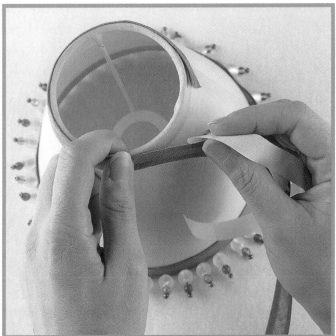

5 Cut a strip of double-sided tape to fit your bias binding. Fix the sticky side to the back of the binding. Start at the back of the lampshade and remove the end of the backing from the double-sided tape. Remove the backing slowly as you attach the tape. Stretch the tape slightly to allow for the shade's contour. Press down firmly all along the edging.

6 Back the remaining piece of bias with double-sided tape and run this along the top rim of the lampshade, allowing a slight overlap. Press down firmly to secure.

Daisy table runner

Beads are a wonderful embellishment to have on a table centrepiece. They catch the eye and can be admired and talked about as your guests enjoy their meal. Here, I've used peach and cream pearls on cream brocade to suit a summer wedding breakfast or similar celebratory meal. Glass beads on richly coloured silk would be luxurious for a special winter dinner. You could even create a Christmas table runner to adorn your festive table.

Measuring 3 cm (1¼ in) in from the edge of your runner, work out the length of beading you will need (see Beads list opposite).

YOU WILL NEED

Pencil

Pins

Table runner

Beading needle

Cotton thread

2 tassels

Head pins

Jewellery pliers

BEADS

For every 5 cm (2 in) of edging (1 daisy stem) you need:

1 flat oval pearl 12 x 9 mm (½ x ⅜ in)

6 flat oval pearls 6 x 5 mm (¼ x ⅜ in) (allow 8 for corner/point flowers)

10 translucent pink rocailles (off-centre holes) size 6/0 (if you can't get off-centre holes, use 8 ordinary size 6/0 beads)

For every 5 cm (2 in) of plain edging, you will need:

1 flat oval pearl 12 x 9 mm (½ x ⅜ in)

18 translucent pink rocailles (off-centre holes) size 6/0 or 15 ordinary size 6/0 beads

For the tassels you will need:

4 pearl drops size 9

2 flat oval pearls 12 x 9 mm (½ x ⅜ in)

2 pearl drops size 4

1 Photocopy or trace the template on page 94 and pin to the table runner. Mark out the pattern with a sharp pencil.

2 Sew each large flat oval pearl into the marked position, alternating the colours. Stitch each one twice through and secure the thread on the underside with a knot.

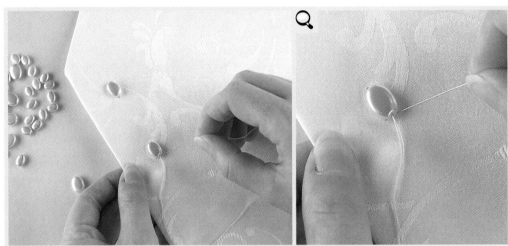

3 Sew the "petals" onto the "flowers". Start by sewing two of the smaller pearls either side of the large one, but in line with the edging. Then fill in, with the others radiating outwards. Use a total of six pearls.

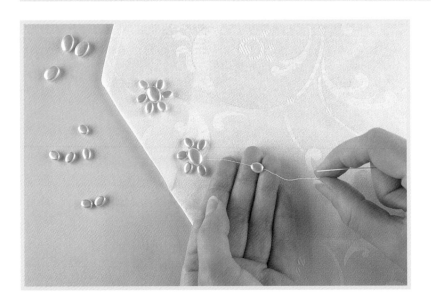

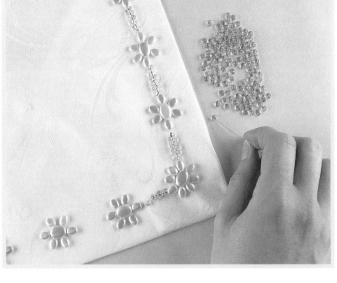

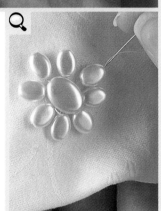

4   When you reach a corner or a point, you may need to add two more petals and alter their arrangement so that the line of rocailles can still run straight to them.

5   Once all your daisies are sewn into position, you can start to link them up using the rocailles. Push your needle through the runner at the tip of a petal point and thread on approximately 10 beads. Push the needle back through at the next petal. Carry on in this way, weaving your needle from front to back until all your daisies are joined up.

6   For the plain edging, first stitch on the large oval pearl. The intervals between them are the same as for the daisy centres. Alternate the colours as before. Then, join them together with strands of rocailles, this time with 18 to a strand (see step 5).

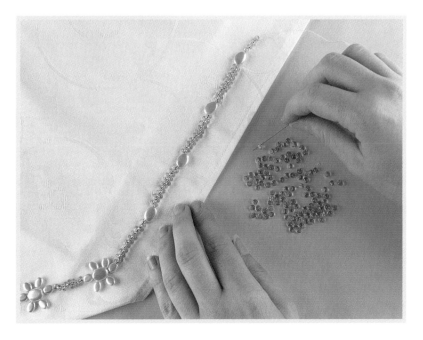

39

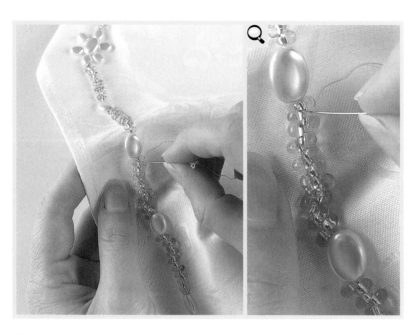

7 Work your way around the runner, couching down the beads to the fabric to secure their position every second or third bead (see step 2, Sewing on beads, page 17).

8 Embellish the tassels with pearls. Thread a size 9 pearl drop onto a head pin, then trim off the excess wire, leaving enough to make a loop. Using your jewellery pliers, make a loop. Hook it onto the head of the tassel at one side and close the loop. Repeat and hook a second pearl drop on the other side of the tassel.

9 Stitch an oval pearl onto the head of the tassel and stitch the tassel onto the cloth's corners. Thread a size 4 pearl droplet between the tassel and the cloth as shown. Repeat steps 8 and 9 to make the second tassel.

Flower bouquet

Grace your table with these lovely delicate flowers, whose heart-shaped droplets hang freely and quiver with movement, bringing them to life. These flowers would make a wonderful birthday or Mother's Day gift that will last forever. The flowers can be formed using beads other than hearts. Try different types to create a unique bouquet.

YOU WILL NEED

Wire cutters

Galvanized wire 0.8 mm

Ruler

Jewellery pliers

Superglue

1 head pin per heart bead

BEADS

1 vial green frosted rainbow bugle size 3'''

1 seed pearl per heart bead

3–6 colour-lined heart beads 8 mm (⅜ in) per flower stem

1 vial green matt striped beads

1 Cut a 22 cm (8¾ in) length of wire. Using your jewellery pliers, make a small loop at the end of the wire.

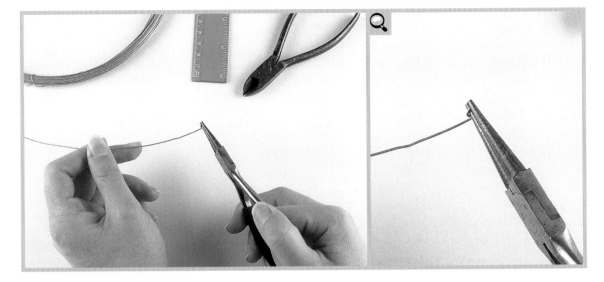

2 Thread on three green frosted rainbow bugle beads.

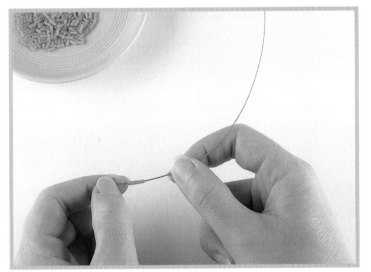

ARTIST'S TIP

Remember to take a sample of wire with you when buying beads to make sure it fits through the hole in the beads.

3 Make a second loop in the wire close to the beads by simply twisting the wire around the nose of the pliers.

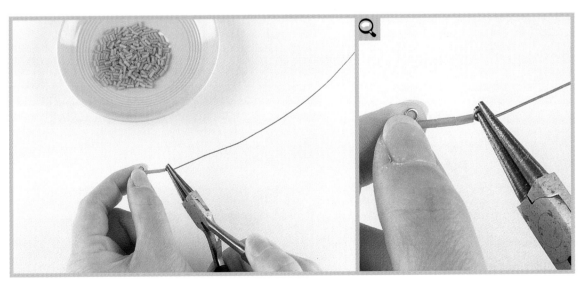

4 Continue in this way, threading on three bugles, followed by a loop in the wire, until you have between three and six loops. Then, fill up the remaining wire with the bugle beads, glueing the last one on.

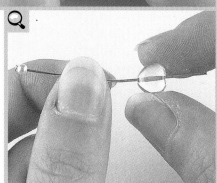

5 To make the flowers, thread a seed pearl bead and a heart bead (pointed end first) onto a head pin.

6 Snip off the excess wire leaving just enough to form a loop at the top of the heart. Don't close the loop (see Suspending beads/Using jewellery head pins, page 14). Repeat to make the rest of the flowers for the stem.

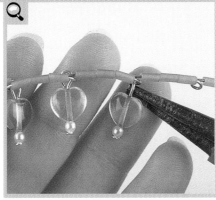

7 Hook each flower in turn onto a wire loop on the stem. Close the flower's loop so that the flower dangles securely from the stem.

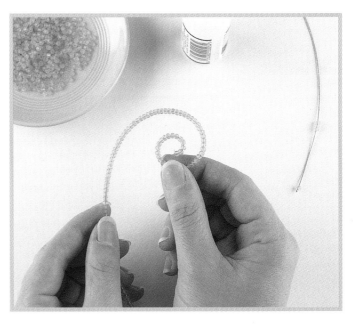

8 To make the leaf fronds, thread varying lengths of wire (18–25 cm / 7–10 in) with striped beads. Glue the top and bottom beads into position and form into spiral fronds.

Alternative design

Colour-lined heart beads are available in a range of colours. Arrange them in individual colours or mix them together. Different coloured hearts can be hung on a single stem.

Wine glass charmers

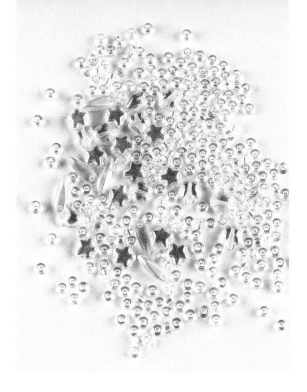

Avoid confusion over whose wine glass is whose. Personalize them with beads, making them beautiful into the bargain. Here, glasses for a bride and groom (or engaged couple) have been embellished with pretty beads including cat's eye heart beads. For the guests, a simple beaded ring has been added to the stems of the glasses (see Alternative design page 50), making a talking point for your guests. You can change the type and colour of the beads used to suit your wedding scheme.

YOU WILL NEED

Memory bracelet wire

Wire cutters

Pencil

Jewellery pliers

Wine glass

Superglue

BEADS

For each charmer you will need:

1 vial transparent rainbow beads size 8/0 (this will be enough for two charmers)

Approximately 40 glass star beads 6 mm (¼ in)

40 pearlized dagger drops

2 white cat's eye hearts 6 mm (¼ in)

Safety note
Take care when wrapping the wire around the glass. Memory wire is sprung, so you need to make sure that you do not allow it to spring back against the glass as there is a danger that the glass may break.

1 You will need approximately five–seven loops of memory wire for each glass. Working with the middle loops, wrap these forcibly around a pencil and form into tight loops with jewellery pliers. Don't worry if they look bent and uneven, they will be fine once they are beaded.

2 Forcibly stretch out this middle section of wire to match the length of the stem of your glasses.

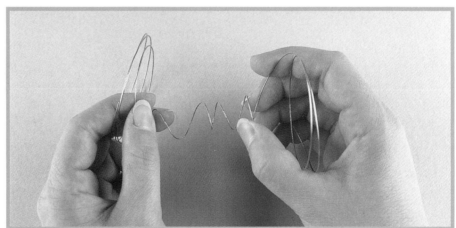

3 Carefully wrap the wire around your glass, taking great care not to let it spring against the glass. You may need to make the top loop slightly tighter to ensure it stays up. You may also need to bend the last loop down so that it lies flat to the glass.

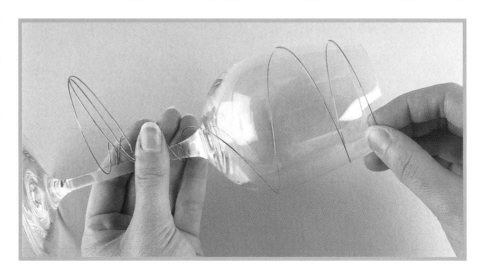

4 Remove the wire from the glass. Thread on the transparent rainbow beads and slide them down to cover the middle section for the stem of the glass. Add a touch of superglue to the bottom bead to stop them sliding any further.

5 Continue threading on the rainbow beads for the top of the glass. Add a decorative bead in between every three rainbow beads. (Alternate the star beads with the dagger drops.)

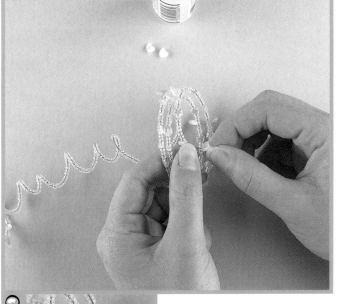

6 Repeat the same bead pattern for the bottom loops. Finish off each end of wire by glueing on a cat's eye heart at either end.

Alternative design

For a simpler option, make these charming stem rings – use different-coloured spacers for each so that your guests will be able to identify their own glasses.

For each glass you will need:

Memory ring wire

8 pressed glass leaves 12 x 7 mm (½ x ¼ in)

9 round beads

Superglue

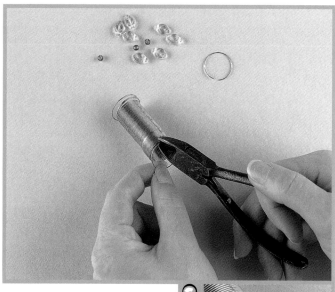

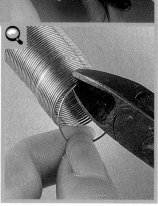

1 For each glass, you need one loop of ring memory wire. Cut firmly; you will have one open ring of wire.

2 Superglue a round bead to the end of the loop. Once dry, alternately thread on beads and leaves until the wire is full. Secure the last bead with superglue.

Napkin rings

These pretty napkin rings are perfect for gracing a spring or summer table. These very decorative items, made with charming flower beads threaded onto beaded wire, are simple to make. You can use the same design to make a lovely bracelet. Use memory wire instead of the galvanized wire. Obviously, you can make the bracelet using beads in the colours of your choice.

YOU WILL NEED
(for each ring)

Galvanized wire 0.8 mm

Wire cutters

Ruler

Jewellery pliers

Child's rolling pin or similar

Superglue

7 head pins

BEADS

1 vial colour-lined rocailles size 6/0

6 light green small lamp bead leaves

6 frosted daisy lamp beads

6 seed pearls

6 pink daisy beads 9 mm (³⁄₈ in)

2 silver foil-lined ridge cone lamp beads 10 x 8 mm (½ x ³⁄₈ in)

1 clear frosted foiled disc bead 10 mm (½ in)

1 Cut a 25.5 cm (20 in) length of wire for each ring. Using jewellery pliers, make a loop at one end. (This will prevent the beads falling off.)

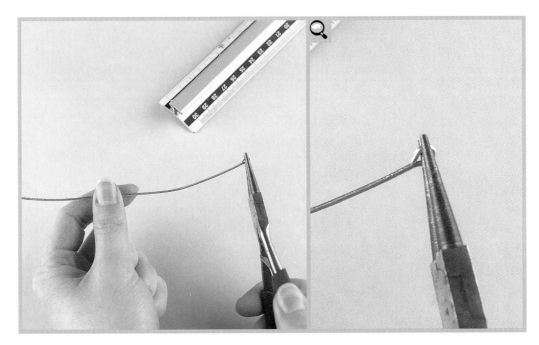

2 Thread on the colour-lined beads and slide them down the wire. Make a loop in the other end.

3 Wrap your beaded wire around the rolling pin firmly so that it forms a spiral.

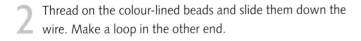

4 Snip off the loop at one end of the wire using wire cutters.

5 Thread on three glass leaves. Splay them out, then add a touch of superglue to hold them in position.

6 Thread on three frosted daisy beads. Space these between the leaves and use superglue to hold them in place.

7 Thread a seed pearl onto each head pin, then thread on a pink daisy bead so that the pearl becomes the centre of the flower. Leave about 1 cm (½ in) wire protruding at the back of the flower and snip off the excess. Using the jewellery pliers, form the wire into a loop.

ARTIST'S TIP

For a winter or Christmas table, choose dark green leaves and red flowers or berry beads.

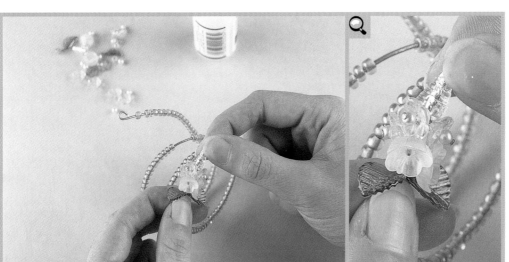

8 Thread the pink flowers onto the ring. Glue them into position if necessary. You should have just enough wire left for your cone bead to fit over. Snip off any excess and glue on the cone bead. Repeat steps 4–8 on the other end of the ring.

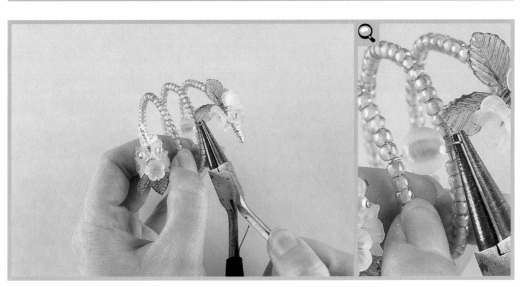

9 Thread a disc bead onto a head pin. Snip off the head of the pin and form a loop with your jewellery pliers at either end of the bead. Insert one loop between a couple of beads on one of the inner coils and close it. Hook the other loop over the adjacent coil and close it.

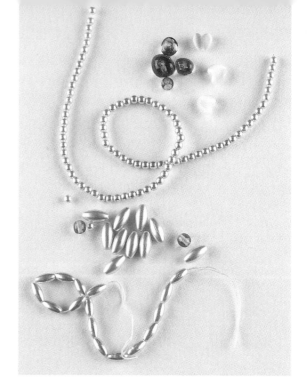

Pretty coathanger

Special occasions warrant special clothes, and special clothes deserve special hangers. Make this charming hanger for your precious wedding dress or favourite evening gown to hang on. Choose a colour that complements the garment and bead as befits the occasion. Here, we have used pearls, pearlized droplets and glass beads to create this pretty hanger. If you prefer, you could create your own design rather than using the pattern template provided on page 94.

YOU WILL NEED

Pencil

Pins

Padded hanger

Cotton thread

Beading needle

Double-sided tape

115cm (45¼ in) thin pale pink ribbon

BEADS

1 string small pink pearls

7 pale blue large pearl cat's eye beads

21 pale blue medium pearl oats

21 pale blue small pearl oats

1 large violet potato bead

3 violet round beads

3 cat's eye hearts

5 small frosted droplets

1 vial rainbow rocailles

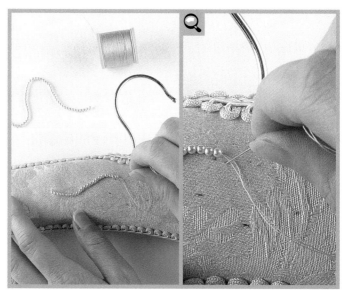

1 Photocopy or trace the template on page 94. Pin the paper onto the hanger and mark the critical points in the design with a sharp pencil, pressing through the paper to make a dot on the hanger.

2 Thread a length of cotton onto the beading needle and make a small stitch at the lefthand edge of the pattern to secure. Thread on 17 small pink pearls. Allow enough slack in the cotton to follow the contour of the stem and attach the end to the hanger by stitching through.

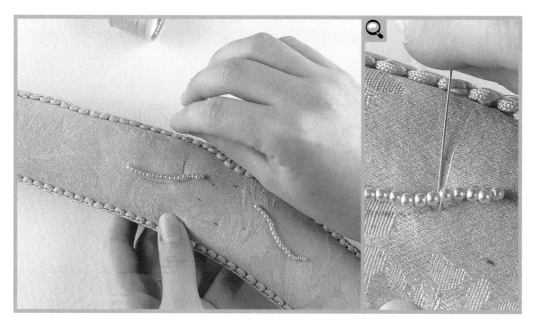

3 Take your needle under the fabric and out at the corresponding place for the opposite stem and repeat. Couch down both stems to secure their positions (see step 2, Sewing on beads, page 17).

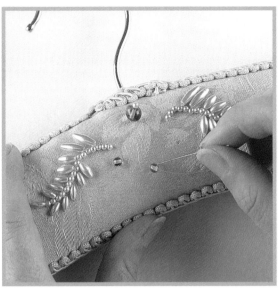

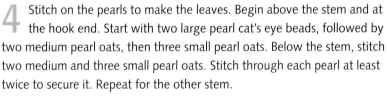

4 Stitch on the pearls to make the leaves. Begin above the stem and at the hook end. Start with two large pearl cat's eye beads, followed by two medium pearl oats, then three small pearl oats. Below the stem, stitch two medium and three small pearl oats. Stitch through each pearl at least twice to secure it. Repeat for the other stem.

5 Stitch the large potato bead in the centre of the top flower. Stitch the violet round beads in the centre of the other three flowers. Once you have got these in position, adding the petals is easy.

6 To make the top flower, stitch on three large pearls radiating downwards from the centre, with two medium ones either side. The other three flowers have six petals, each radiating from the centre.

7 When the flowers are completed, extra small pink pearls can be added to the ends of each leaf. Then rainbow rocailles can be stitched on here and there to add a touch of finesse.

8 To complete the design, add hearts at the top of either side of the top flower and beneath the central lower flower. Stitch frosted droplets to the ends of each leaf and below the three lower flowers.

9 Cut a thin strip of double-sided tape. Stick it along the outside edge of the hanger's hook. Measure in 10 cm (4 in) from one end of the ribbon. Starting at this point, stick the ribbon from the bottom of the hook to the top. Then, wind the excess ribbon around the hook from the top to the bottom.

10 Complete the binding at the base of the hook and tie the ends to make a neat bow. This can be done with a different-coloured ribbon if preferred.

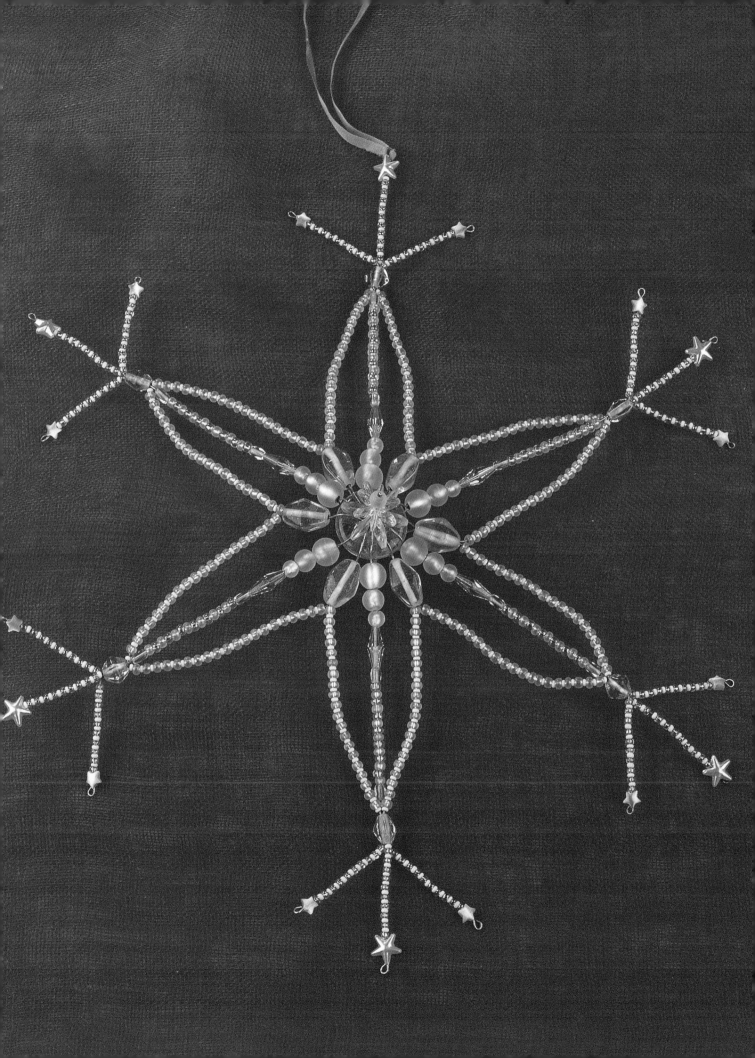

PROJECT (11) *Snowflake*

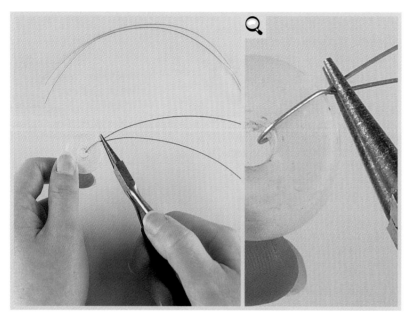

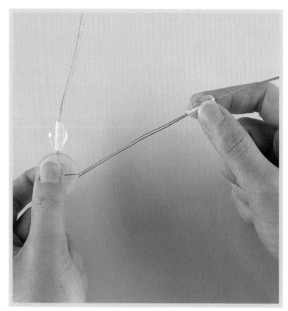

1 Measure and cut 6 lengths of wire 40 cm (16 in) long and 6 lengths 21.5 cm (8½ in) long. Thread one of the longer strands through the hole in your centre disc bead, pulling the wires together so that they double up. Squeeze the wires together at the edge of the bead using jewellery pliers.

2 Thread a second, 40 cm (16 in) strand of wire on, doubling up as before. Thread a large lozenge bead onto each doubled strand, pushing them as near to the centre bead as possible.

3 Splay out the pairs of wires and thread each of the four strands with an alternated line of white and frosted silver-lined rocailles, using 20 of each for each strand. Once one strand is completed, loop the end of the wire over, to prevent the beads falling off. Each of these beaded strands will make a side to one of the points of the snowflake.

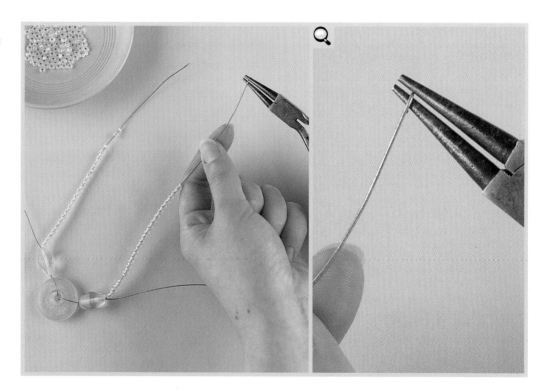

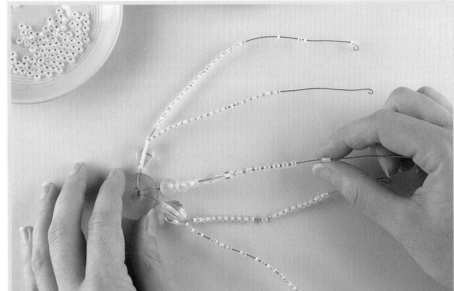

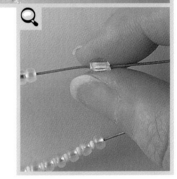

4 Position one of the shorter wire strands between these beaded wires. Double up only the first 3.7 cm (1½ in) and onto this doubled-up section thread on three frosted beads (one of each size), largest first. If any of the doubled wire protrudes, snip off the excess.

5 Now thread the following beads onto the single strand of wire: a faceted crystal bi-cone, a clear pellet bead, then alternate seven frosted silver-lined rocailles and the larger rainbow rocailles. Finish with another pellet bead.

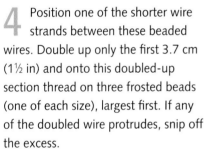

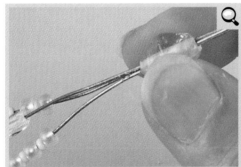

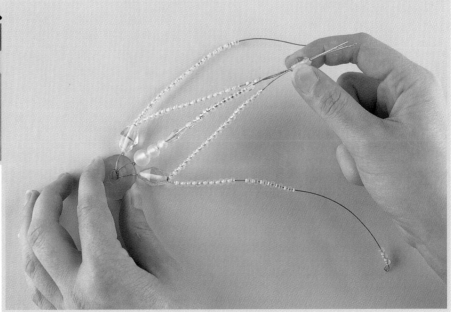

6 Bring together the three central wires and unite them by threading on a small lozenge bead, pushing it up to the existing beading.

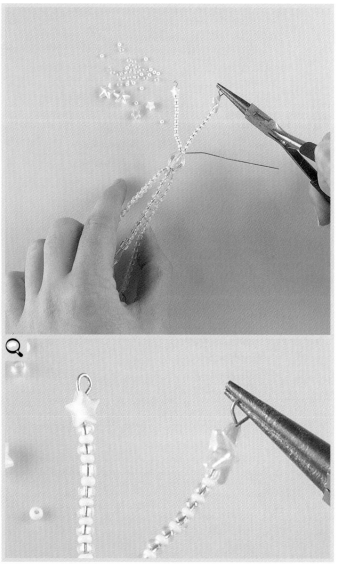

7 Splay out these three top wires from the lozenge bead. The remaining wires should be approximately 5 cm (2 in) in length. Snip off any excess. Thread each strand in turn with white and rainbow rocailles (both size 8/0), using approximately 10 of each. Finish the outer strands with a small cat's eye star and the central one with a larger pearlized star. Loop over each end to secure the beads. You have now completed one of the points of the star. Repeat steps 1–7 to create the other five points, remembering that you already have the beginnings of two left over from step 3.

8 Once the points of the snowflake are complete, add beads to the centre to hide the wires on the disc bead. Using a head pin, thread on a small frosted bead, followed by a small sunburst and then a larger sunburst. Thread this through the central disc bead and repeat the bead sequence in reverse on the other side. Pull the wire tight and form a small loop at the end to secure the beads.

Antique lampshade cover

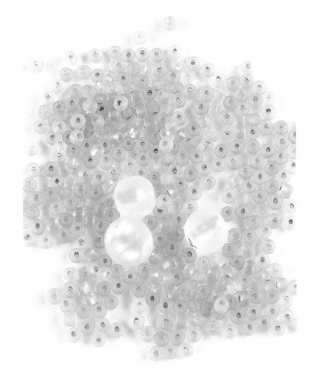

These frosted white antique-effect beads have been threaded onto fine galvanized wire, which has been bent and twisted into loops and scallops to make a frame that fits over a golden lampshade. The base circumference of the lampshade used in the project is 45.5 cm (18 in). If your shade is a different size, then you will need to adapt the design to fit. For a more contemporary look, choose a red shade with purple beads.

YOU WILL NEED

Galvanized wire 0.8 mm

Wire cutters

Jewellery pliers

BEADS

500 g (1 lb 2 oz) frosted silver-lined seed beads 0.6 mm (⅓ in)

11 frosted foil disc beads

1 Thread 638 seed beads onto the roll of wire. Make a loop in the end of the wire. Allow an extra 15 cm (6 in) of wire after the beads and cut the wire. Make another loop.

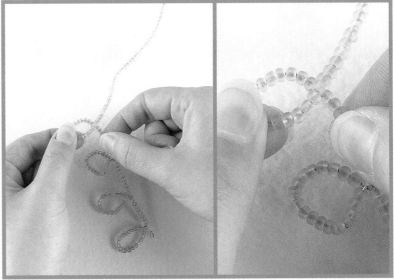

2 Each loop "petal" is comprised of 21 beads, and between each petal there are eight beads. Count along eight beads and slide these beads along to make a slight gap in the wire. Then count 21 beads, create a slight gap in the wire and form these beads into a loop around your finger. Twist the bare wire together to form a petal. Continue to make petals with eight-bead intervals.

3 Once you have formed 22 petals, open one of the loops and join the wires together, closing the loop to secure. (If after forming the petals you have excess wire, just cut it off and make another loop.)

ARTIST'S TIP

It's better to use too much wire than too little, as any excess can easily be cut off.

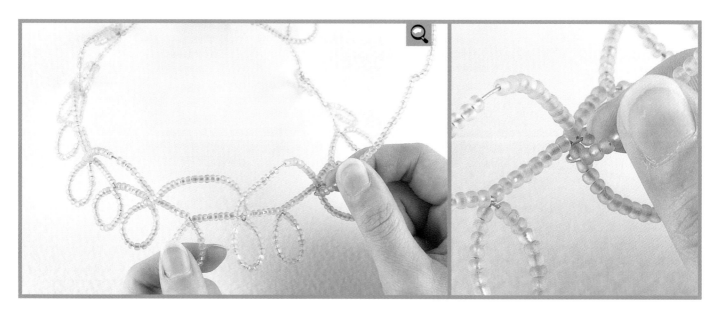

4 Thread up another length of wire with 264 seed beads. Again, allow for slack at the end before cutting the wire. Form this wire into scallops with 24 beads to each. Attach these by making a space between the beads at the end of each

scallop and twisting the wire around the neck of one of the petals. Skip a petal, then secure the end of the scallop to the next petal. Continue until you have worked your way round. This completes the bottom of the lampshade decoration.

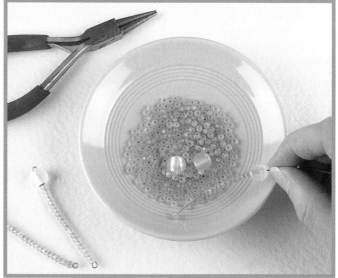

5 Form a circle of beaded wire to fit around the top of the lampshade. Allow 1 cm (½ in) of slack. Form a hook at one end of the wire and an eye at the other. Use jewellery pliers to secure the ends together. Make sure the beads aren't too tightly packed together, as you will need to attach beaded struts to this circle later on.

6 Cut 11 lengths of wire 5 mm (¼ in) longer than the height of your shade. Take one length of wire. Make a hook at one end, then thread on a disc bead followed by seed beads. Make another hook. These beaded struts connect the top circle and the bottom decoration together.

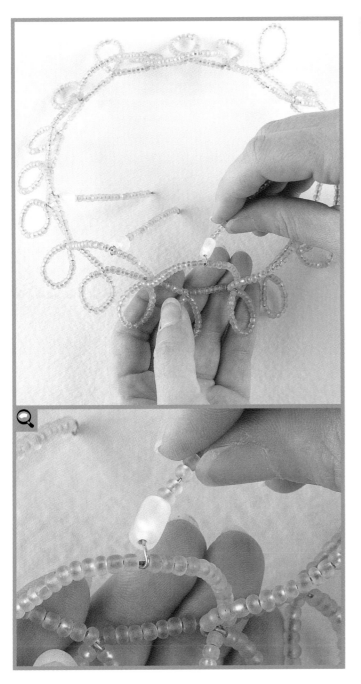

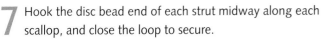
7 Hook the disc bead end of each strut midway along each scallop, and close the loop to secure.

8 Count the beads on the top circle and divide by 11. This figure is the number of beads between each strut. Attach each strut, closing the loop with jewellery pliers.

Butterfly cushion

A beaded butterfly motif has been added to the corners of this beautiful silk cushion, personalizing it and turning it into an extremely fashionable home accessory. Make a few cushions to scatter over a sofa or bed, each with a different butterfly design. When designing your own butterflies, it is best to fold your paper in half and draw and cut out the butterfly from that centre fold so that the wings are symmetrical. Alternatively, use a flower, bird or berry motif. The same motif can be added to a throw or even slippers to fully complement your décor.

YOU WILL NEED

Pencil

Silk cushion

Pins

Embroidery hoop (optional)

Beading needle

Cotton thread

Silver thread

BEADS

1 disc lamp bead 10 mm (½ in)

1 oval lamp bead 23 x 6 mm (1 x ¼ in)

10 mauve dagger drops

Seed bead mixture (pearly blues, silver, rainbow finished, silver-lined etc.)

2 flat diamonds

4 pearl oats size 3/0

4 hearts 10 mm (½ in)

12 iridescent sequins

10 blue dagger drops

2 faceted crystals 3 mm (⅛ in)

Silver bugles

26 stars AB coat 6 mm (¼ in)

1 Photocopy or trace the template on page 94. Pin the template to the corner of the cushion and trace around it faintly with a pencil. For the subsequent steps it is important that you do not stitch through both layers of fabric. To make sure, have one hand inside the cover or use an embroidery hoop if you have one.

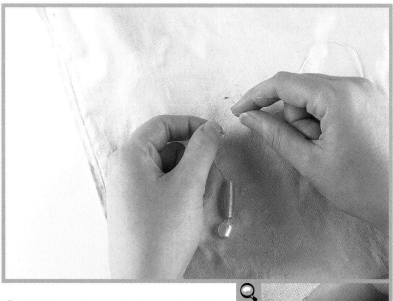

2 Stitch on the centre beads: the disc lamp bead for the head, the oval for the body and a mauve dagger for the tail. Stitch through each bead several times to secure to the silk. Be sure to stitch through only one layer.

3 Thread up a long strand of doubled cotton. Knot the ends together and stitch through from the inside of the cushion. At the neck of the butterfly, thread on a medley of seed beads, until there is enough to shape the wings and central loop. Then, secure the thread at the tail end of the butterfly.

4 Begin from the neck of the butterfly to couch down the wings. Do this by bringing the needle through from the back every second or third bead, and stitch over the beaded thread and back through. This will hold the shape of the wings. Keep these stitches very small so that they don't show (see step 2, Sewing on beads, page 17).

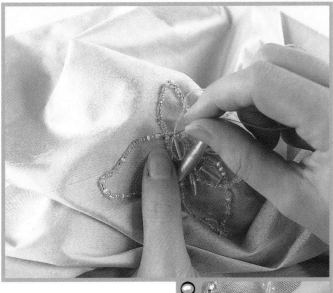

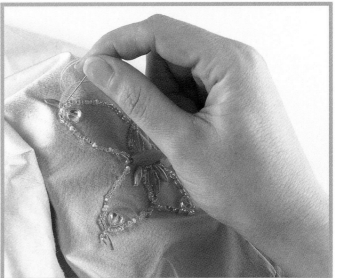

5 To embellish the wings, insert a flat diamond bead into each loop. Stitch these on securely. Then add pearl oats in each wing, radiating them outwards from the body, each pointing to the wing tip.

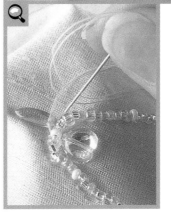

6 At the tip of each wing add a heart, stitching them securely in position, with the pointed end fitting into the wing tip. Then add a blue dagger drop to the tip of each base wing.

7 Using a double strand of silver thread, stitch a pair of antennae for the head. Do this by making a single stitch for each from head to tip, leaving it loose enough to follow the curve of the form, then couch down with ordinary cotton thread to secure and shape. Add a small crystal bead to the tip of each antenna.

8 From the tip of each pearl oat bead to the tip of each wing, stitch on a line of sequins. Bring the needle up through the centre of the sequin, thread on a seed bead and return the needle back through the sequin's hole. The bead will hold the sequin in place.

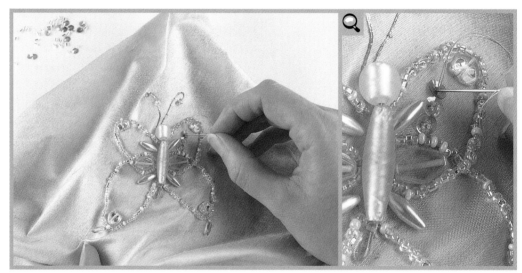

9 Radiating out from the sequinned centre line of each wing, stitch on dagger drops, blue ones on the outside, mauve on the inside. You may need to secure the ends of the daggers with a little cross stitch over each end.

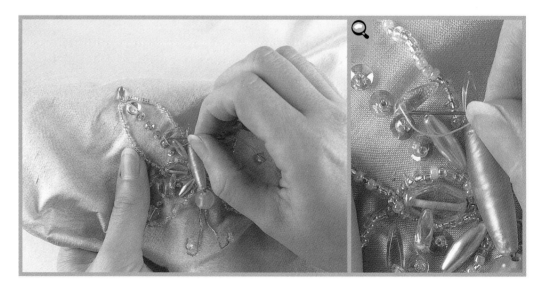

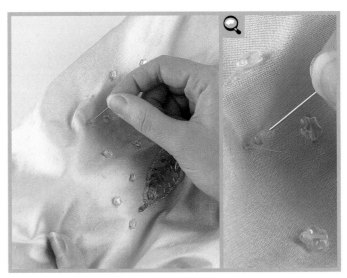

10 Bugles can be used as infill for any spaces left. Look at the photo on page 79 for guidance.

11 Once the butterfly is finished, stitch tiny stars all around it in that corner of the cushion. Try to make the spacings fairly regular and symmetrical so that they look slightly random without being messy.

Alternative design

Play around with a selection of beads on some double-sided tape to create interesting designs. Keep more expensive or special beads as the centre points for the body and head of the butterfly. This design is simple yet effective.

Silk cushion

For this project I have chosen a cushion that opens midway, making it easy to stitch the beaded ribbon along the opening. The two-tone ribbon perfectly complements the elegant silk cushion, making it a very fashionable accessory. You could coordinate a lampshade or throw to match.

The cushion used in this project is 40.5 cm (16 in) square.

YOU WILL NEED

Silk cushion (with midway zip or opening)

Ribbon (to fit width of cushion plus 5 cm / 2 in excess)

Ruler

Pins

Beading needle

Cotton thread

Scissors

BEADS

1 vial colour-lined purple/blue rocailles size 6/0

1 vial colour-lined purple/blue Z-cut delicas

32 oily navy blue rocailles size 6/0

20 flower beads

16 turquoise Indian lozenge beads 5 mm (¼ in)

32 amethyst-coloured Austrian crystal beads 4 mm (⅛ in)

1 vial oily purple rocailles size 11/0

18 purple miracle beads

20 green Indian lozenge beads 5 mm (¼ in)

12 amethyst-coloured potato beads 4 x 6 mm (⅛ x ¼ in)

2 purple lamp beads

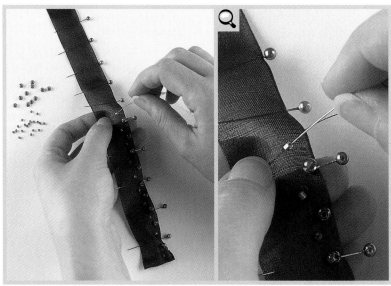

1 Lay the ribbon across the cushion. Measure in 2.5 cm (1 in). From this point measure, and mark with a pin, 2 cm (¾ in) intervals along the ribbon. The fringe is made up of two different styles of bead strand.These pins mark the position for the flower bead strands. The other style of strand hangs in between.

2 Take the ribbon off the cushion. Firstly stitch the colour-lined purple/blue rocailles on the edge of the ribbon. Stitch at roughly 1 cm (½ in) intervals, but you don't need to measure this. Stitch the Z-cut delicas 6 mm (¼ in) in from the edge positioned in between the rocailles.

3 To create the fringing, overstitch along the edge of the ribbon until you reach the first pin. To make the first bead strand, thread the following onto the needle: an oily navy blue rocaille, a flower bead, a turquoise lozenge bead, a crystal bead and an oily purple rocaille. Thread the needle back through the beads to the ribbon (the last bead will now hang sideways). Overstitch until you reach the midway point between the two pins. Now stitch the second bead strand. Thread the following onto the needle: an oily navy blue rocaille, a miracle bead, a green lozenge bead, a crystal bead and an oily purple rocaille. Thread the needle back through the beads to the ribbon and overstitch until you reach the next pin. Continue alternating the bead strands until you've decorated the whole ribbon.

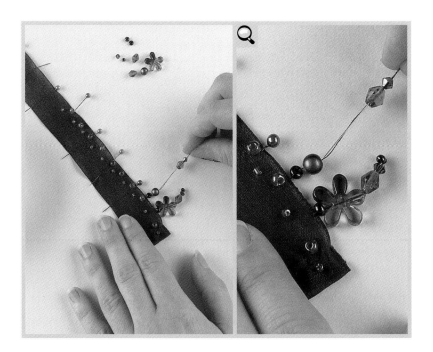

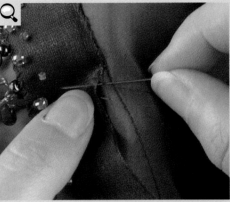

4 When you have completed your fringing, stitch back the raw edges at either end of the ribbon. Then attach the ribbon across the edge of the opening flap of the cushion.

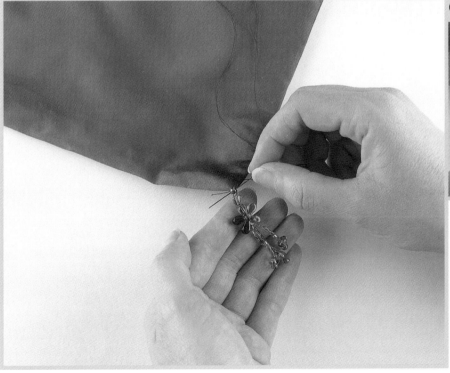

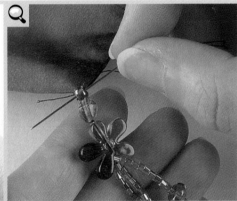

5 There are two different styles of tassel on the cushion. See page 16, Making a tassel, for one style. Make the second style in exactly the same way, except use a miracle bead, a lamp bead and a green lozenge bead for the body of the tassel. Stitch the tassels securely to the corners of the cushion.

Candle ring

Gazing into candlelight is always captivating, and even more so when there are beads that will glimmer and glisten when they catch the light. The suspended droplets will respond to vibration, bringing the surround to life.

This design can be easily adapted for bigger or smaller candles or holders. Just enlarge or reduce the instructions accordingly. The candle ring used in the project has a 9 cm (3½ in) bowl and a 2.5 cm (1 in) hole for the candle.

YOU WILL NEED

Galvanized wire 0.8mm

Wire cutters

Ruler

Jewellery pliers

Floristry wire

Superglue

BEADS

17 top drilled lustre-finish droplets

1 vial small transparent rainbow seed beads

9 pink potato beads

9 hearts (lustre-finish) 10 mm (½ in)

18 stars 6 mm (¼ in)

18 droplets: 9 white / 9 mauve frosted drops 6 x 9 mm (¼ x ⅜ in)

18 clear white frosted silver-lined rocailles

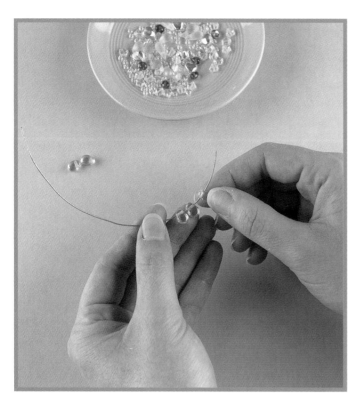

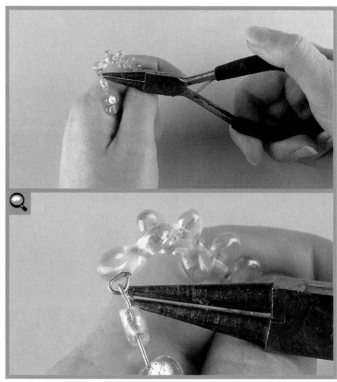

1 Cut a 13 cm (5¼ in) length of galvanized wire and thread on 17 lustre droplets.

2 Form a hook at one end and an eye at the other with your jewellery pliers. Interlock them, closing the loop (see Joining wire ends, page 15). Make sure the beads are not too tightly squeezed together. This will form the base circle of the net ring.

3 Cut 17 lengths of floristry wire 25 cm (10 in) long. Fold each in half by pulling with the pliers as shown.

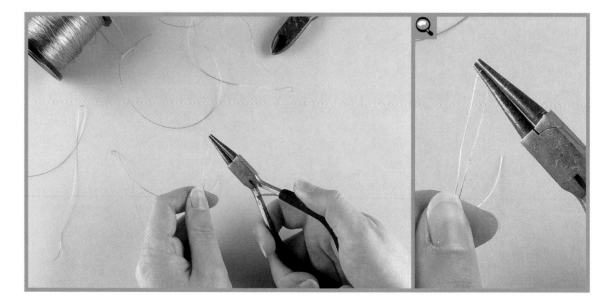

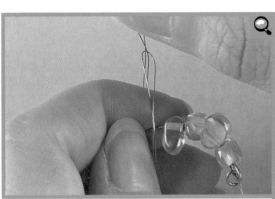

4 Wrap the folded ends of the floristry wire around the galvanized wire between each bead on the base circle. Then, thread the ends of the floristry wire through their own loop and pull to interlock the wire close to the beads. Repeat in between the next few beads. It's best to work in small sections rather than attaching all of the wires at the same time.

ARTIST'S TIP

After threading on each section of beads, fold the wires down to prevent the beads falling off while working on other sections.

5 Thread two rainbow seed beads onto each wire. These create the beginnings of the beaded net.

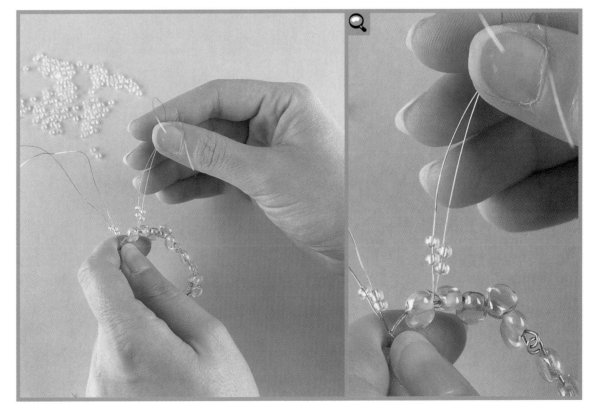

6 Splay out the wires and pair up the adjacent wires, taking one length from one piece of floristry and one length from another. Thread a pink potato bead on the first pair. Measure up 2.5 cm (1 in) from the base circle and glue the bead in position.

7 Thread a heart bead onto the second pair. Again, measure up 2.5 cm (1 in) from the base circle and glue the bead in position. Repeat steps 4–7 all the way around, alternating the heart and potato beads.

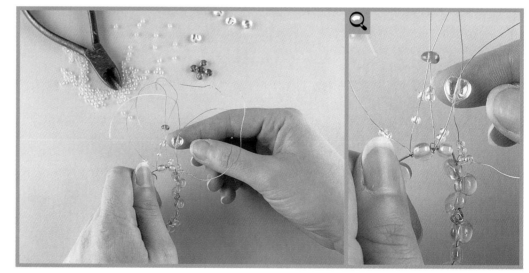

8 Splay out the wires again from the hearts and the potato beads. Thread another two rainbow seed beads on each strand, then bind back into pairs with a star bead. Continue all the way round.

9 Splay out the wires again and add another two rainbow beads on each wire. Then attach the droplet beads by threading a pair of wires through the holes in opposite directions as shown. Alternate the colours of the droplets.

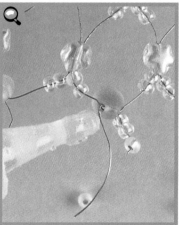

10 Finally, glue a couple of frosted rocailles onto the ends of each wire and trim off any excess wire. Dab glue here and there to space out all the rainbow beads on the net.

Templates

Pretty Coathanger (pages 56–60)

Butterfly Cushion (pages 78–83)

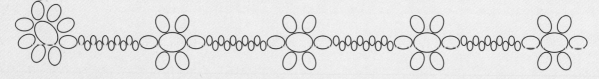

Daisy Table Runner (pages 36–40)
Enlarge this template using a photocopier set to 141%
or use the common A4 to A3 setting.

Suppliers

UK

Bead Exclusive
Nixon House
119–121 Teignmouth Road
Torquay
Devon TQ1 4HA
Tel: 01803 322 000
www.beadexclusive.com
General bead supplies. Mail order.

The Bead Shop
21A Tower Street
London WC2H 9NS
Tel: 020 7240 0931
Mail order tel: 020 8553 3240
General bead supplies. Shop and mail order.

The Bead Shop
Tel: 0115 9588899
www.mailorder-beads.co.uk
General bead supplies. Shop and online mail order.

Beads Direct
3 Birch Lea
East Leake
Loughborough
Leicestershire LE12 6LA
Tel: 01509 852187
www.beadsdirect.co.uk
General bead supplies. Online mail order.

Constellation Beads
Tel: 01833 621094
www.constellationbeads.co.uk
General bead supplies. Online mail order.

Creative Beadcraft Ltd
(Ells and Farrier)
Tel: 020 7629 9964
www.creativebeadcraft.co.uk
General bead supplies. Shop and mail order.

Jules Gems
Tel: 0845 123 5828
www.julesgems.com
General bead supplies. Online mail order.

Kernowcraft Rocks and Gems Ltd
Tel: 01872 573888
www.kernowcraft.com
General bead supplies. Mail order.

USA

Auntie's Beads
Tel: 866-26BEADS (toll free)
www.auntiesbeads.com
Online and phone ordering. Stores in Dallas, Houston and Kansas City areas.

Beadbox
Tel: 1-800-BEADBOX
Retailer of beads and components. Three stores in the USA. Shop online.

Michaels
Tel: 1-800-6424235
www.michaels.com
Retailer of arts and crafts materials. Stores throughout the USA and Canada. Shop online.

South Africa

Beadcrazi
68 Eighth Avenue
Morningside 2057
Tel: 031-3038107

Bead Empire
109 Fifth Street
Wynberg
Sandton 2196
Tel/fax: 011-7862693

Beads & Findings Wholesale
18 Pafuri Road
Emmarentia
Johannesburg 2195
Tel: 011-8882136

Craft Distributors
(mail order service available)
203 Long Street
Cape Town 8001
Tel: 021-4234687

Lions Square Crafter's Shop
150 Main Road
Somerset West 7130
Tel: 021-8517308

New Zealand

Beadazzle – Bead Creations
(nationwide)
www.beadazzle.co.nz

The Bead Hold
161 Pt Chev Road
Pt Chevalier
Auckland
Tel: 0-9-845 1345

Fun Beads Ltd
28 Ngapipi Road
Orakei
Auckland
Tel: 0-9-524 4864

String of Beads
23 Liardet Street
New Plymouth
Tel: 0-6-759 6985

Craft Warehouse – Bead Me Up
Hinemoa Street
Rotorua
Tel: 0-7-349 0844

Beads & Components for
 Jewellery
81 Ward Street
Upper Hutt
Tel: 0-4-977 2639

Beyond Beads
288 Cuba Street
Wellington
Tel: 0-4-384 1525

The Bead Shop
66 Stanley Street
Queenstown
Tel: 0-3-442 3239

The Bead Shop
7 The Octagon
Dunedin
Tel: 0-3-477 7420

Australia

ACT

Beads Etc.
Shop 1, 61 Dundas Court
Phillip ACT 2606
Tel: (02) 6282 9441
www.beadsetc.com.au

NSW

The Bead Company of Australia
324 Forest Road
Hurstville NSW 2220
Tel: (02) 9580 4923
www.beadcompany.com.au

(Other stores at Chatswood, Enmore and Penrith)

NT

Beadazzled
Shop 1, 4 Rowling Street
Casuarina NT 0810

QLD

Bead, Trimming & Craft
Company
39 Merivale Street
South Brisbane QLD 4101
Tel: (07) 3844 5722
www.beadtrimmingcraft.com.au

SA

Bead Hive
Citi Centre Building
Shop 42, Pulteney Street
Adelaide SA 5000
Tel: (08) 8223 5773
www.beadhive.com.au

TAS

The Bead Company of Tasmania
120 Elizabeth Street
Hobart 7000
Tel: (03) 6234 6380

VIC

Beads & Buttons Galore
187 High Street
Prahran VIC 3181
Tel: (03) 9510 5477
www.beadsandbuttonsgalore.
com.au

Bizzarr Beads
285 Swanston Street
Melbourne VIC 3000
Tel: (03) 9663 8662
Mail Order Tel: (03) 9329 8496
www.bizzarrbeads.com.au
(Other stores at Highpoint City, Chadstone, Doncaster and Knox City)

WA

The Bead Company
3/205 Alexander Road
Belmont WA 6104
Tel: (08) 9478 4868
www.beadco.com.au

Index